BLUEPRINTS OF TOMORROW

Designing Software for Generations Ahead

Abdulhafeez Bello

Blueprints of Tomorrow: Designing Software for Generations Ahead

Published in Nigeria in 2021 by Plexity Digital

A catalogue record of this book will be available from the National Library of Nigeria.

Table of contents

Preface

When I first started writing Blueprints of Tomorrow: Designing Software for Generations Ahead, I asked myself what it meant to build something that would last. Too often, the world of technology is obsessed with quick deadlines, releases, and iterations. However, history has shown that the most meaningful creations are those that endure overtime rather than those that dominate a single moment.

This book explores how we can design software with the same tenacity. It is not a syntax or frameworks manual, as those will eventually fade. Instead, it is an investigation into the principles that persist resilience, adaptability, imagination, and responsibility. I wanted to create a work that speaks to more than just coders but also to thinkers, dreamers, and digital stewards.

Each chapter was written from the perspective that software is inextricably linked to society. Code decisions have far-reaching consequences for culture, the economy, and human relationships. As a result, every architect of tomorrow bears a responsibility not only to solve technical problems but also to protect values that transcend technology itself. These pages contain stories about balance: between automation and humanity, between efficiency and meaning, and between innovation and legacy. You will see education reframed as a lifelong pursuit and imagination emphasized as essential rather than optional. My hope is that as you read, you will think about not only the systems you build but also the futures you create.

This preface serves as an invitation to ask questions rather than an introduction to answers. What do we leave behind? How will future generations remember our work? And what role can we play in ensuring that software becomes not a disposable tool but an enduring gift? If these questions strike a chord with you, you are the intended audience for this book. May its words challenge, inspire, and remind you that in the digital age, every line of code contains echoes of the future.

Foreword

In a time when technology advances rapidly, it's easy to mistake progress for permanence. Each decade produces new tools, frameworks, and paradigms, only for them to fade into obscurity as the next wave arrives. Yet despite this relentless pace, one truth remains constant: the systems we create today will influence the lives of future generations. This book, Blueprints of Tomorrow: Designing Software for Generations Ahead, contributes to that conversation with clarity, urgency, and vision. What makes this work compelling is its refusal to reduce software to mere lines of code or fleeting trends. Instead, it presents software as cultural infrastructure like libraries, bridges, and philosophies that outlast their creators. Abdulhafeez Bello approaches software design not just as a technical task but as a moral and generational duty. His writing reminds us that code is not only functional but also consequential. This book doesn't just provide prescriptions for better design; it encourages us to think differently. It urges us to view education as lifelong, automation as partnership, and innovation as stewardship. It challenges us to resist the lure of short-term gains and instead develop systems with adaptability, resilience, and purpose.

As you progress through these chapters, you will encounter not only strategies but also reflections that delve deeper than the surface of technology. You'll be prompted to ask: Who benefits from what we build? Who bears the costs of what we neglect? And what will remain once we are gone? Abdulhafeez Bello has crafted more than a guide for software architects; he has written a manifesto for future builders. His words resonate far beyond programming, speaking to anyone who dares to dream of lasting legacies. If you are holding this book, you are already part of that journey. The question is no longer whether tomorrow will come but what it will inherit. May this work inspire you to create systems not just for now but for the countless generations yet to come.

Introduction

Every generation inherits tools from the past and builds the foundations for the future. The printing press transformed knowledge. The steam engine reshaped economies. Electricity redefined the boundaries of possibility. Today, software has become our defining infrastructure. It is the invisible architecture of modern civilization, powering commerce, communication, education, governance, and even the way we imagine ourselves.

Yet, unlike bridges or cathedrals, software often feels transient. Products rise and vanish within a few years. Programming languages surge and fade. Companies scale rapidly and collapse just as quickly. In this environment, it is easy to think of technology as disposable, built only for the moment. But this mindset risks leaving behind fragile foundations for the generations that follow. This book was born from the conviction that software must be designed not just for today but for tomorrow. As a software engineer, I have witnessed how small technical decisions can ripple outward in unpredictable ways. An overlooked security vulnerability can cause cascading harm. A thoughtfully designed interface can empower millions. These experiences taught me that designing software is not only a technical responsibility but also a generational one. We are not simply solving problems for the present; we are shaping the possibilities of the future.

The chapters ahead invite you to step back and consider software as more than code. It is culture. It is policy. It is memory. It is the shared blueprint upon which generations will construct their lives. And if that is true, then we must design with humility and foresight. We must think about resilience, about adaptability, about ethical responsibility, and about legacy.

In the pages that follow, you will find reflections on human-centered design, longevity in code, artificial intelligence, ethics, sustainability, and global collaboration. You will be asked to imagine software not as an isolated product but as part of a larger fabric that connects generations. You will also be invited to wrestle with difficult questions:

How do we create systems that endure beyond our lifetimes?

How can we balance the speed of innovation with the responsibility of care?

What values must we embed in the technologies we pass forward?

And ultimately, what kind of digital legacy do we want to leave?

This book is not about frameworks, libraries, or programming syntax. Those change with the seasons. Instead, it is about principles that can guide us across time. Just as architects design buildings with both immediate utility and long-term stability in mind, so too must software engineers design systems that are both useful today and adaptable for tomorrow. One of the most important themes in this book is humility. We cannot predict the future with certainty, nor can we control how the tools we create will be used. But we can design with awareness, embedding openness, transparency, and adaptability into our work. We can design systems that invite reinterpretation rather than enforce rigidity. We can design in ways that acknowledge that the next generation may know better than we do. At its heart, *Blueprints of Tomorrow: Designing Software for Generations Ahead* is both a challenge and an invitation. It is a challenge to resist the pull of short-termism and instead cultivate a mindset of stewardship. And it is an invitation to participate in a conversation that transcends the boundaries of the present to see we as part of a lineage of builders, shaping not just tools but futures. If you are a software engineer, a designer, a technologist, or simply someone curious about how technology shapes human destiny, this book is for you. It asks you not only to think about the systems you create but also to consider the stories those systems will tell long after you are gone. The future is not something that happens to us, it is something we design. And the blueprints we draft today will become the architecture of tomorrow. Let us draw them with wisdom, care, and vision.

Chapter 1

The Dawn of Future Software

The story of software begins not with silicon, electricity, or even machines, but with imagination. At its core, software is nothing more than structured thought, a detailed and precise form of logic that machines can understand and execute. To write software is to translate the most abstract dreams into a new way to communicate, a method to analyze data on a massive scale, and a means to create art into an executable, tangible reality. From the earliest punch cards used to program Charles Babbage's mechanical designs in the 19th century to the high-level abstractions of modern programming languages, the fundamental impulse has remained the same. It is the human drive to build, to solve, and to shape the future that truly endures, far more than any specific line of code.

We often describe software as a tool, but this definition is far too small and too confining. A hammer is a tool that assists in the task of driving nails. A compass is a tool that helps in the task of navigation. While both are invaluable, they are static. They perform a single function with unwavering consistency. Software, however, is fundamentally different. It evolves and adapts. It possesses a dynamic quality that hammers and compasses do not. Software can learn, scaling to handle unprecedented volumes of data and new challenges. It communicates across vast networks, replicating itself and weaving into new contexts. It infiltrates domains that its original creators never foresaw, transforming finance, medicine, and art in ways that defy simple categorization. The dawn of future software is not about the emergence of new utilities; it is about the profound recognition that software has become a force of civilization as vital as law, language, and art. It is a new medium through which human intention is manifested on a global scale. This is a philosophical shift, not merely a technological one. We are no longer just building tools; we are building the very foundations of our future societies.

The seeds of innovation rarely appear as a sudden flash of lightning. Instead, they germinate in obscure soil, often unnoticed or dismissed until they have grown too large and powerful to ignore. Consider the origins of the internet: a Cold War experiment, conceived as a decentralized network designed for resilient military communication in the face of a nuclear attack. The initial project, ARPANET, was a network connecting a handful of research institutions. At its inception, few of its architects could have imagined that their work would one day become the nervous system of global society, connecting billions of people and shaping the very fabric of culture, commerce, and politics. The seeds planted in secrecy for a very specific military purpose have blossomed into one of the most transformative phenomena in all of human history, a testament to the unpredictable nature of true innovation.

This same pattern holds true for countless other software breakthroughs. The electronic spreadsheet, for example, was initially conceived as a specific tool for accountants to model financial statements. Its creators, Dan Bricklin and Bob Frankston, saw a niche need for a digital version of the traditional ledger. Yet, the flexibility and power of the spreadsheet model its ability to easily calculate and recalculate values based on inputs, propelled it far beyond its original intent. Today, spreadsheets underpin the planning of businesses, the budgets of governments, and the personal finances of individuals worldwide. Similarly, the first smartphone operating systems were designed to enable basic calls, texts, and simple applications. They were meant to be convenient extensions of existing communication devices. But this platform became the stage on which entire industries were born and destroyed. The seeds of app stores, mobile banking, on-demand ride services, and social media platforms were all contained within the simple premise of a portable, connected computer. Innovation is inherently unpredictable and therein lies its beauty and its peril. The software of tomorrow will likely emerge from the peripheries, from experimental projects, and from daring imaginations that see beyond the immediate horizon. It is a constant reminder that we must cultivate a culture of curiosity and experimentation, for we never know which seemingly small idea will become the next great paradigm shift.

But if history teaches us anything, it is that these seeds of innovation do not merely grow; they multiply. Software's growth is not linear but exponential. A single breakthrough breeds a thousand new possibilities, each one a potential starting point for further innovation. The invention of the World Wide Web provided a platform, but it was the subsequent creation of search engines, social media, and e-commerce that truly defined its impact. Today, we are witnessing the emergence of artificial intelligence models that can generate images, text, and music from simple prompts. This is a monumental breakthrough in human creativity and problem-solving. But tomorrow, these same models may design their own successors, creating recursive spirals of innovation that move at a pace beyond our current comprehension. The models could begin to optimize themselves, to learn and adapt in ways that we cannot even fully predict, let alone control. The dawn we are witnessing is not a gentle sunrise but a blazing eruption, a flood of new possibilities pouring over the old boundaries and reshaping the landscape of technology and society. This exponential growth presents a unique challenge and a profound responsibility, forcing us to consider the long-term implications of our creations with a level of foresight never before required.

Today's Code, Tomorrow's Legacy

Every programmer knows the enduring paradox of legacy code: it is at once a treasure and a burden. On one hand, legacy code is the lifeblood of our digital world. It keeps businesses alive, sustains critical infrastructure, and holds decades of accumulated knowledge and business logic. It is the code that performs the mission-critical functions that we take for granted every day. On the other hand, it is often fragile, difficult to maintain, and resistant to change. It is built on outdated architectures, written in languages that are no longer common, and its original creators have often long since moved on. What we call "legacy" is, in truth, yesterday's innovation, persisting into today and shaping tomorrow.

This reality should sober us. The code we write today will inevitably become someone's inheritance tomorrow. A line written in haste to meet a deadline, a technical debt taken for quick deployment, a shortcut that seems harmless in the moment, these choices may linger in critical systems for decades. They can shape decisions, influence outcomes, and in the most extreme cases, even determine life or death. Think of the software controlling aircraft navigation, which must be perfectly reliable.

Consider the code embedded in medical devices that monitor patients and deliver life-saving treatments. Think of the complex systems that manage our energy grids, which must operate flawlessly to prevent widespread blackouts. These systems are not disposable; they are designed to endure, often far longer than their creators imagined. They are the digital cathedrals of our age, built to withstand the test of time, even as the technological landscape shifts dramatically around them.

This endurance forces us to profoundly reconsider our responsibility as software creators. We must begin to think not in terms of product cycles or quarterly releases, but in terms of generations. Just as the architects of ancient cathedrals in Europe built with the knowledge that their work would outlast them, so too must software designers and engineers embrace the reality that their creations may form the foundational infrastructure of societies they will never see. These medieval builders often never lived to see their work completed. Yet they carved their stones with incredible care and precision, embedding beauty and permanence into places that only future generations would see and appreciate. They worked not for immediate glory, but for posterity, for a purpose far greater than themselves.

What would software look like if we approached it with that same devotion to permanence and craft? What if we designed not only for functionality and efficiency but also for meaning, resilience, and grace? This is not a call for perfection, which is an impossible and paralyzing goal. It is a call for a shift in perspective. It means we should prioritize clarity and maintainability, so future generations of developers can understand and build upon our work. It means we should embrace open standards and modular designs that can be adapted and integrated with new technologies. It means we should document not just the "what" of our code but also the "why" and the reasoning behind key architectural decisions that might seem obvious today but will be completely opaque tomorrow. This shift in mindset is about more than just a clean codebase; it is about building a legacy of thoughtful, enduring work that serves humanity for the long haul.

Why Tomorrow Demands More

The pace of technological change today surpasses anything in recorded history. Where once it took centuries for fundamental tools like the plow or the printing press to evolve, revolutions in software and hardware now occur within years or even months. In this hyper-accelerated context, designing software for tomorrow requires not just technical skill but a profound level of visionary thinking. The systems we create are no longer isolated to screens and servers; they are embedded in the very fabric of human life, shaping our daily existence in ways both subtle and profound.

Think of the hospital ward where complex machines monitor patients in real time, processing vast streams of data to guide doctors to make life-saving decisions. The software in these systems is not just a tool; it is a direct participant in the act of healing. Think of the satellite constellations mapping our planet, informing agriculture, guiding disaster response, and enabling global navigation. This software is the invisible hand that makes our modern world function. Think of the digital classrooms where children in remote villages can learn alongside peers in bustling cities across the globe. This software is a bridge to opportunity and a catalyst for social change. In all these cases, software is not peripheral; it is central. To design poorly in this context is not simply a technical flaw; it is a human cost. A glitch in a medical device, a bug in a navigation system, or an error in a financial algorithm can have catastrophic real-world consequences, affecting lives, livelihoods, and entire communities.

Tomorrow demands software that is inclusive by design, sustainable at its core, and adaptable to technologies not yet imagined. Inclusive design means creating systems that are accessible to everyone, regardless of ability, background, or circumstance. It means building for diversity from the outset, rather than trying to patch on accessibility as an afterthought. Sustainable software means writing efficient code that minimizes its energy footprint, recognizing the immense power consumption of global data centers and the urgent need to address climate change. And adaptability means designing systems that can endure shocks and evolve with changing requirements and remain relevant even as the world shifts beneath them. This requires building systems with open architectures and clear interfaces, avoiding proprietary lock-in, and prioritizing flexibility over rigid, monolithic structures.

Above all, tomorrow demands humility: the recognition that no single individual can foresee all outcomes and that collaboration across disciplines, cultures, and generations is essential. The complex problems of the future, from climate change to global health, will not be solved by siloed thinking. They will require engineers working alongside ethicists, designers working with sociologists, and business leaders collaborating with policymakers. We must move beyond the idea of the lone genius programmer and embrace a more collaborative, holistic approach to creation.

The philosophical awakening we are experiencing is perhaps the most critical dimension of this new era. We must recognize that software is never neutral. It is not just a collection of instructions. It encodes values, assumptions, and worldviews. Every choice, from the design of an interface to the architecture of a system, reflects a vision of how humans should interact with technology and with one another. When we decide how algorithms rank search results, we are not just organizing information; we are shaping access to knowledge and influencing the very nature of truth. When we determine how social platforms display content, we are not just optimizing for engagement; we are influencing culture, identity, and even political stability. When we optimize code for efficiency, we make decisions about energy consumption, climate impact, and sustainability. The choices we make are not merely technical; they are always, implicitly or explicitly, moral.

This realization compels us to think more deeply about the kind of future we wish to create. The dawn of future software is not a passive event; it is an invitation to responsibility. To design for generations ahead is to accept that we are shaping not just systems, but societies. We are building the foundations of a new civilization, and the choices we make today will echo for decades to come.

At this moment, humanity stands at a crossroads. We can continue to build disposable software patchwork systems designed for immediate profit, quick deployment, and short lifespans. This path is familiar, comfortable, and often rewarded in the short term. Or we can begin to craft blueprints of permanence, systems designed to serve generations, resilient against both technical decay and social disruption. The crossroads is not hypothetical; it is present in every design decision, every architectural choice, and every ethical consideration. When a startup chooses speed over stability, when a corporation chooses profit over sustainability, when a developer chooses convenience over inclusivity, the future is being written in that moment, and the short-term view is prevailing. Conversely, when engineers pause to ask, "How will this serve not only my users today but also their children tomorrow?" the future shifts toward resilience and wisdom.

The dawn of this new era is not something that happens to us; it is something we choose to embrace. And like every dawn, it brings both light and shadow, promise and peril. The coming chapters of this book will explore these dimensions in more detail, but for now, we must settle into this profound truth: the software of tomorrow is already being born in the lines of code we write today. The question is not whether it will shape the future; it will. The only remaining question is whether we will shape it wisely. The power is in our hands, but so is the responsibility. It is time for us to build not just with speed, but with soul.

Chapter 2

Human-Centered Design for Generations

If the dawn of future software begins with imagination, its guiding principle must be people. Code is not written in a vacuum; it is written for someone, somewhere, with needs, limitations, and dreams. Yet, in the rapid evolution of technology, it is easy to lose sight of this fundamental truth. Too often, software is built to impress venture capitalists, to chase fleeting market trends, or to dominate a specific sector, while the lived realities of the human beings who will use it fade into the background. This myopic focus on metrics over meaning can lead to brilliant technical achievements that are, paradoxically, utterly devoid of human wisdom. The future we are designing will either elevate and enrich human experience or reduce it to a series of hollow transactions. The choice lies in whether we embrace human-centered design not as a fleeting trend or a marketing buzzword, but as the very soul of software architecture for generations ahead. This is a call to move beyond the transactional and into the transformational.

Beyond Functionality: Designing for Lives

The simplest definition of software design is the arrangement of systems and interfaces to accomplish a specific set of tasks. But this definition ignores the deeper, more profound truth: every single design choice, no matter how small, touches a human life. A login screen is not just a credential checkpoint; it is either an inviting gateway or a frustrating barrier. A medical app is not merely a data collector; it is either a source of vital reassurance and empowerment or a generator of crippling anxiety and confusion. A payment platform is not simply a digital ledger; it is either a bridge to opportunity, allowing small businesses to thrive and families to send money across borders, or it is a gatekeeper of exclusion, denying access to those who lack the "right" type of documentation or technical literacy. The consequences of these design decisions ripple far beyond the screen.

When we speak of designing for generations, we are not designing for abstract "users" or a faceless "target audience." We are designing for the children who will grow up in worlds shaped by our decisions, their cognitive and social development influenced by the very interfaces we create today. We are designing for grandparents who may depend on intuitive, accessible interfaces to stay connected with their families and manage their health. We are designing for communities that will lean on our software to organize, to educate, to mobilize, and to thrive. Functionality, of course, matters immensely; a system that doesn't work is useless. But if that functionality is not paired with a deep sense of compassion and foresight, we risk building systems that are technically efficient but profoundly inhuman. They will accomplish their task but fail their users.

Consider how powerfully design shapes human memory itself. The social platforms we use today determine what moments are preserved, how they are framed, and how they are recalled. The simple "like" button, seemingly innocuous in its appearance, has transformed how self-worth is measured for millions of people worldwide, particularly younger generations. A seemingly minor design choice rippled outward into culture, affecting confidence, identity, social dynamics, and even political discourse. When software can influence how humans remember their own lives, when it can curate their past and define their present, the stakes of design are no longer merely technical; they are existential. This is the weight of the responsibility we carry: we are building the digital archives of human life. The question is, will they be compassionate archives or cynical ones? Will they be designed to celebrate our shared humanity or to exploit our vulnerabilities?

Empathy as Architecture

Empathy is often misunderstood as a "soft skill," something secondary to the "hard" science of engineering, relegated to the realm of user experience designers rather than core to a system's architecture. But in truth, empathy is a profound architectural principle. To design with empathy is to anticipate not just how a system will function, but how it will *feel* to the people who interact with it. It is to recognize the fears, hopes, limitations, and strengths of those who will use the system and to embed those recognitions into the very blueprint itself. This isn't about making a system "nice"; it's about making it fundamentally more robust and resilient.

For instance, consider the practice of accessibility. A visually impaired user navigating a website does not merely need compliance with a checklist of technical standards; they need a design that respects their dignity and understands their experience. This means building accessibility not as an afterthought or a quick fix but as a foundational element of the design process. It means ensuring text-to-speech compatibility, intuitive keyboard navigation, and seamless interaction are as much a part of the core architecture as a database or an API. The same principle applies to designing for children, which demands not only simplicity but also robust protection, ensuring their digital environment is safe, nurturing, and free from exploitation.

Designing for empathy is, in essence, designing for humanity itself, its fragility, its resilience, and its incredible diversity.

Empathy as architecture also requires acknowledging and embracing diversity in its broadest sense. Not all cultures use technology in the same way or hold the same values about privacy, community, and personal expression. A color that symbolizes prosperity and good fortune in one culture may symbolize mourning and death in another. A design pattern that feels intuitive in the West, with its emphasis on individual control, may feel alien in the East, where collective harmony is often prioritized. If future software is to be generational, it must also be global. Empathy, then, is not just about understanding individual users, it is about understanding entire civilizations and their complex cultural tapestries. The most visionary software designers will not be those who master the most complex algorithms or build the fastest systems. They will be those who master the human imagination and its infinite variations. They will ask: How does this design affirm human dignity across different cultures? How does it expand opportunity rather than restrict it? How does it adapt not just to new technologies but to the evolving story of humanity itself?

Inclusive by Default

The final and most crucial test of human-centered design is inclusion. The history of technology, unfortunately, is riddled with examples of exclusion of systems designed for the majority while ignoring the margins. In the early days of voice recognition software, for instance, datasets were heavily biased toward male voices, leading to notoriously poor performance for female users. This wasn't a malicious choice but a failure of imagination and a lack of inclusive data collection. Similarly, early translation systems focused on major languages with large economic markets, excluding hundreds of minority languages because they were deemed "unprofitable." People in rural or impoverished regions were excluded from early internet access because infrastructure investment favored densely populated urban centers with a higher return on investment. These exclusions were not just technical oversights; they were profound social inequities baked into the very fabric of our digital world.

If we are to design software for generations ahead, we cannot afford these exclusions. Inclusion must not be an add-on, a checkbox to be ticked after the fact, but a default setting, a core architectural principle. This means designing systems that assume diversity rather than treating it as an exception. It means building platforms that serve not just the most common languages but hundreds of them, recognizing the linguistic heritage of billions of people. It means creating interfaces that adapt across literacy levels, educational backgrounds, and physical and cognitive abilities. It means ensuring that connectivity is not a luxury afforded only to the wealthy but a right accessible to all, through resilient, low-cost, and widely available technology.

Generational design asks us to imagine not only the user in front of us but also the user yet to be born and the user in a context we cannot currently comprehend. What needs will a teenager in a rapidly urbanizing city in Nairobi have thirty years from now? What will a farmer in rural India require when climate patterns shift and their livelihoods depend on real-time data? What tools will an elderly person in Tokyo need to remain connected to their family in a century where lifespans may stretch far longer than we can imagine today? Inclusion is not simply about diversity in the present; it is about continuity and adaptability in the future. It is about ensuring that the software of tomorrow can evolve and adapt to the ever-changing and unpredictable human story.

The Heart of Generational Design

When software historians look back centuries from now, they may not marvel at the technical specifications of our systems. The specific architectures, the programming languages, and the processing speeds will appear as primitive to them as the early punch cards and command lines of the 20th century appear to us today. What they will marvel at or critique is whether we had the wisdom to design with humanity at the very center. Did we create systems that outlast the noise of markets and the fleeting whims of trends? Did we prioritize compassion over short-term profit, human dignity over speed, and long-term resilience over immediate convenience?

Human-centered design is not a luxury. It is the very foundation of building software that can stand the test of generations. Without it, tomorrow's systems will be brittle, exclusionary, and hollow, built on a foundation of sand. With it, they can become enduring structures of connection, empowerment, and meaning, built on a foundation of rock. The dawn of future software demands that we move beyond thinking of design as merely pixels and patterns on a screen. It calls us to see design as a moral act, a generational promise, and an architectural blueprint for the human experience. In the chapters that follow, we will explore the technical, ethical, and cultural implications of this profound calling. But it all begins here, with the fundamental recognition that every line of code we write is also a line in the story of humanity. The question we must all face is: what story will we choose to write? Will we tell a story of exclusion and apathy, or one of empathy and enduring purpose?

Chapter 3

Longevity in Code

When we speak of permanence in the digital age, the conversation often seems ironic. After all, nothing seems less permanent than technology. Phones become obsolete within a few years, operating systems are abandoned, platforms rise and fall with dizzying speed, and even the languages we use to program are replaced by shinier tools. The culture of software has taught us to accept disposability as the natural order. Yet, as civilization increasingly relies on digital infrastructure, the stakes of disposability grow higher. If tomorrow's hospitals, power grids, education systems, and global economies depend on code, can we afford to build them with the same fragility as consumer apps?

Longevity in code is not merely about writing software that lasts; it is about writing software that *endures with dignity*. It is about treating systems not as disposable artifacts of commerce but as cultural infrastructure, carrying the memory and trust of generations. Just as cathedrals, libraries, and bridges were built to last, so too must the software of tomorrow. For if digital architecture collapses every few decades, society will forever be rebuilding on unstable ground.

Writing for Centuries, Not Versions

The first step in imagining longevity is to rethink our relationship with time. Today, software is largely governed by the tyranny of release cycles. Quarterly updates, annual overhauls, and rapid product launches create an environment where code is valued for speed more than for stability. Startups are taught to "move fast and break things." But when what we are building underpins hospitals, flight systems, financial institutions, and communication platforms, breaking things is no longer a sign of progress; it is a betrayal of trust.

Consider COBOL, a programming language designed in 1959. Critics scoffed at its verbosity and simplicity, yet it endures more than six decades later, silently powering banks, insurance systems, and government infrastructure. Billions of financial transactions every day depend on a language that predates the moon landing. COBOL's longevity is not an accident. It was designed to be readable, adaptable, and understandable by non-specialists, a principle that gave it resilience across generations.

Contrast this with the graveyard of frameworks and languages abandoned after only a few years. These may have been technically brilliant, but brilliance without clarity does not endure. Longevity favors humility over cleverness. It favors simplicity that invites stewardship over complexity that dazzles but alienates. The lesson is clear: to write for centuries is to resist the temptation of novelty for novelty's sake and to build with the patience of those who know they are creating an inheritance.

The Case for Self-Healing Architectures

If longevity is the dream, resilience is the craft. Over time, all systems decay. Bugs accumulate, vulnerabilities emerge, dependencies break, and the weight of complexity grows heavier. Traditional approaches rely on human maintenance patches, updates, and rewrites. But as systems become more critical and interdependent, relying solely on human oversight becomes insufficient. The software of the future must not only function it must *heal itself*.

Imagine a hospital network running millions of medical devices, each connected to a central system. In today's world, a minor bug in one component could cascade, creating outages with life-threatening consequences. But in a self-healing architecture, the system detects anomalies, isolates failing components, reroutes operations, and applies corrective patterns automatically, all while keeping the hospital operational.

We already see glimpses of this in cloud infrastructures where servers scale up or down dynamically, or in databases that automatically replicate and repair themselves across regions. But these are the earliest steps. The future will demand systems that adapt not only to technical failures but also to social, environmental, and political disruptions. A logistics platform of the future may autonomously reroute supply chains in response to a natural disaster. An education platform may dynamically adjust to different cultural contexts and learning styles across generations. Longevity requires this kind of adaptive resilience software that refuses to collapse.

But resilience must be tethered to accountability. A self-healing system that evolves without oversight risks creating opaque black boxes. Longevity without transparency is dangerous. Thus, the future must balance autonomy with explainability, ensuring that healing does not obscure understanding.

Designing Systems That Outlast Teams

Perhaps the greatest enemy of longevity is not time but turnover. Teams disband. Companies fold. Governments shift. Knowledge evaporates. The code that remains is often cryptic, undocumented, and brittle. Inheritance becomes a curse rather than a gift.

There is a story, often told in whispers among engineers, of a single programmer who retired from a government agency, taking with him the knowledge of a system that had been running for decades. When the system failed, no one knew how to repair it. Millions of dollars were spent trying to understand code that had been written with brilliance but no generosity. This is the cautionary tale of shortsightedness. Longevity requires writing code not for us but for strangers we will never meet. It requires humility, the acknowledgment that our clever tricks may confuse rather than enlighten, that our undocumented brilliance may one day become a nightmare for another.

Readable code, thorough documentation, and generous design are acts of stewardship. They are gifts for the future. They acknowledge that teams will dissolve, companies will vanish, but software will persist. The question is: will it persist as a foundation or as a ruin? Open-source communities provide a model. Projects like Linux, maintained for decades by shifting generations of contributors, prove that stewardship can outlast any individual or company. The lesson here is not only technical; it is cultural. Longevity thrives where communities take ownership, where knowledge is shared rather than hoarded, and where systems are treated as commons rather than property.

The Paradox of Longevity

Some argue that longevity in code is futile. Technology evolves so rapidly, they say, that writing for centuries has been impossible. Why bother designing for permanence when new paradigms will make today's systems irrelevant? The answer lies in distinguishing between *tools* and *principles*. Languages may change, and frameworks may fade, but principles of clarity, adaptability, and stewardship are timeless. A program written in an obsolete language may be rewritten, but if its design embodies clarity and modularity, it will be easier to translate and evolve. Longevity does not mean freezing systems in amber; it means embedding timeless principles into their DNA. Think of language itself. English today is not the English of Shakespeare nor the English of Chaucer, yet continuity persists. The grammar evolves, the vocabulary shifts, but the essence endures. In the same way, software must evolve without severing its lineage. Longevity is not about resisting change; it is about ensuring that change does not erase memory.

Futuristic Scenarios: Code as Civilization's Memory

To truly grasp longevity, we must stretch our imaginations forward. Consider the possibility of interstellar colonies a few centuries from now. Communication between Earth and Mars will take minutes, perhaps hours. In such a world, software will not be updated weekly from headquarters. It will need to endure autonomously, adapting to conditions never anticipated by its creators. Longevity will not be a convenience; it will be survival. Or consider archives of human knowledge encoded in software. Future historians may not turn to dusty books but to living systems of code that preserve the wisdom of our age. If those systems are brittle, future generations may lose vast portions of cultural memory. If they are resilient, they will carry our stories, science, and art across centuries. There is even the possibility that future civilizations will inherit abandoned systems from our era. Much like archaeologists piecing together fragments of ancient cities, they will study our code. The question is, will they find ruins or legacies? Will they see in our systems the marks of hubris and short-term thinking, or the fingerprints of foresight and care?

Toward Generational Software

Longevity in code is not merely a technical challenge; it is a moral imperative. It is the recognition that we are not building only for ourselves but for generations yet unborn. It calls us to resist disposability, to embrace stewardship, and to design with humility and patience. The builders of cathedrals carved their stones knowing they would never see the finished work. We, too, must write code with that devotion, aware that the systems we design may outlast us, shaping societies we will never inhabit. This is the paradox and the promise of longevity: that by writing with patience, humility, and vision, we give the future not just code but continuity, not just systems but inheritance. In the end, longevity is not about resisting time. It is about partnering with it.

Chapter 4

Artificial Intelligence as a Co-Designer

The story of design has always been a story of collaboration. No great cathedral, bridge, or digital system has ever been the product of a single mind alone. Ideas flow through teams, across generations, shaped by dialogue and shared vision. The Gothic architects of Notre-Dame built upon Roman foundations; the engineers of the Brooklyn Bridge drew from centuries of accumulated knowledge; the creators of the internet wove together insights from telecommunications, computer science, and human psychology. Each breakthrough emerged from the fertile ground of collective intelligence.

Now, in the twenty-first century, we stand on the threshold of a new kind of collaboration. For the first time, our partners in design are not only human but also artificial. Artificial intelligence, once regarded as a mere tool, a sophisticated calculator or a pattern matcher, is stepping into the role of a co-designer, a companion in creativity, structure, and vision. This transformation represents more than technological advancement; it signals a fundamental shift in how we conceive, create, and refine the digital systems that shape our world.

This chapter explores the rise of AI as a collaborator rather than a replacement, the responsibilities that come with this partnership, and the possibilities it opens for software that transcends what either humans or machines could create alone. We will examine how this collaboration unfolds in practice, the challenges it presents, and the profound implications for the future of digital design.

Machines That Imagine

For most of computing's history, machines were obedient but unimaginative servants. They computed with perfect accuracy, executed instructions with unwavering precision, and stored information with infinite patience, but they never conceived, never dreamed, never leaped beyond the boundaries of their programming. Creativity, intuition, and innovation, these were the exclusive domains of human consciousness, protected by what seemed an unbridgeable gap between silicon and soul.

Yet today's AI systems compose symphonies that move listeners to tears, generate artwork that challenges our understanding of beauty, write stories that capture the complexity of human experience, and propose scientific hypotheses that advance our knowledge of the universe. They do not merely process information; they synthesize, combine, and transform it in ways that surprise even their creators. In software design, this capacity for imagination is nothing short of transformative. AI can analyze vast repositories of code millions of lines written across decades and identify patterns that would take human teams' years to discover. It can recognize architectural motifs that optimize efficiency, accessibility, and resilience simultaneously, proposing structures that balance competing demands with an elegance born from processing countless examples.

Consider the complexity of modern web applications. A single interface must work seamlessly across devices of different sizes, accommodate users with varying abilities, load quickly on slow networks, remain secure against evolving threats, and feel intuitive to people from diverse cultural backgrounds. The permutations of requirements create a design space so vast that human designers, no matter how skilled, can explore only a fraction of the possibilities.

AI transforms this limitation into an opportunity. Where human designers might consider dozens of layout variations, AI can evaluate thousands. Where a team might test a handful of interaction patterns, AI can simulate the behavior of entire user populations. It can identify solutions that exist in the intersections between disciplines, drawing insights from psychology, physics, biology, and art to create interfaces that feel both familiar and revolutionary. This capacity to "imagine" solutions on a scale is not about replacing human creativity but about expanding it exponentially. Like a telescope that reveals previously invisible stars, AI reveals design possibilities that were always present but beyond our perceptual reach. It serves as both a microscope and a map, helping us see the intricate details of user behavior while simultaneously showing us the broader landscape of design opportunity. The partnership works like improvisation in music, where two skilled musicians create something, neither could achieve alone. The human brings vision, intent, and emotional intelligence, understanding not just what users need but what they hope for, fear, and aspire to become. The AI brings computational power, pattern recognition, and the ability to explore vast solution spaces without fatigue or bias toward familiar approaches.

Together, they produce designs that possess both human warmth and machine precision, systems that feel deeply personal yet perform at a global scale. The AI might propose a novel way to organize information that reduces cognitive load by 40%, while the human ensures that this efficiency serves genuine human needs rather than abstract optimization metrics.

The Dance of Human-AI Collaboration

The emergence of AI as a co-designer has fundamentally altered the rhythm and flow of the design process. Traditional design workflows often followed predictable patterns: research, ideation, prototyping, testing, and refinement. While these phases remain valuable, AI introduces new possibilities for parallel exploration, rapid iteration, and serendipitous discovery. In this new collaborative model, design becomes a continuous dialogue between human intuition and machine analysis. A designer might begin with a rough sketch or a simple statement of intent, "create an interface that helps elderly users manage their medications safely." The AI, drawing from its knowledge of user interface patterns, accessibility research, cognitive psychology, and pharmaceutical safety protocols, can instantly generate dozens of initial concepts, each exploring different approaches to the challenge. But the magic happens in the conversation that follows. The human designer examines these proposals not as final solutions but as starting points for deeper exploration. They might notice that one concept introduces an interaction pattern they hadn't considered, while another suggests a visual metaphor that could be powerful if refined. The designer provides feedback, not just "this works" or "this doesn't," but nuanced guidance about emotional tone, cultural sensitivity, and underlying values.

The AI learns from this feedback in real-time, adjusting its understanding of the project's goals and constraints. It might be discovered that "safety" in this context means not just preventing medication errors but also preserving the user's sense of autonomy and dignity. This insight then influences every subsequent suggestion, creating a feedback loop that becomes increasingly sophisticated and contextually aware.

This collaborative process excels at bridging the gap between ideation and implementation. Traditional design often suffered from a chasm between beautiful concepts and technical reality. Designers would create elegant mockups only to discover that the underlying code structure couldn't support their vision, leading to compromises that diminished the final product. AI co-designers can evaluate both aesthetic and technical feasibility simultaneously, suggesting designs that are not only beautiful but also buildable.

The speed of this collaboration is remarkable. Where traditional design cycles measured progress in weeks, AI-assisted design measures it in hours or even minutes. This acceleration doesn't lead to rushed decisions but rather enables deeper exploration. Designers can pursue multiple directions in parallel, comparing approaches that would have been impossible to explore within conventional timelines. Yet speed is perhaps the least significant advantage. More profound is the way AI collaboration changes the nature of design thinking itself. Working with AI encourages designers to be more explicit about their assumptions, more systematic in their exploration, and more open to unexpected connections. The AI's vast knowledge base often reveals connections between disparate fields, showing how insights from game design might improve financial interfaces or how principles from architecture might enhance data visualization.

Collaboration, Not Replacement

The fear that AI will replace human designers reflects a fundamental misunderstanding of what design truly encompasses. While AI can generate interfaces, optimize layouts, and even create aesthetically pleasing compositions, true design is about far more than solving functional problems. It is about asking the right questions, understanding unspoken needs, and embedding meaning, values, and human dignity into systems that will shape how millions of people live, work, and connect. This distinction becomes clearer when we examine real-world design challenges. Consider the development of a healthcare application designed with AI assistance. The system might analyze thousands of successful health interfaces and propose optimized layouts that reduce user errors and increase engagement. It might suggest color schemes that improve readability, interaction patterns that accommodate motor impairments, and information architectures that minimize cognitive load.

These are valuable contributions, but they represent only one dimension of the design challenge. A human designer must grapple with questions that no algorithm can answer: Does this interface make patients feel empowered or infantilized? Does it respect cultural differences in how people relate to healthcare? Does it balance the efficiency demands of medical professionals with the emotional needs of worried families? These questions require not just data analysis but empathy, cultural understanding, and ethical reasoning. The most effective human-AI design teams recognize these complementary strengths and structure their collaboration accordingly. AI excels at handling scale, exploring vast possibility spaces, identifying patterns across large datasets, and optimizing for measurable outcomes. It can process user behavior data from millions of interactions, identify subtle usability patterns that human observers might miss, and suggest improvements based on statistical evidence rather than assumptions.

Humans bring different but equally essential capabilities: the ability to understand context and meaning, to empathize with user emotions and motivations, to navigate ethical complexities, and to envision futures that don't yet exist. They can interpret the space between what users say they want and what they actually need, understand the political and cultural implications of design decisions, and ensure that technological capabilities serve human flourishing rather than mere efficiency. This partnership works best when both parties understand their roles clearly. The AI becomes a powerful research assistant, pattern detector, and option generator, capable of rapidly exploring design spaces that would take human teams' months to investigate. The human becomes the curator, interpreter, and ethical guardian, ensuring that the resulting designs serve authentic human needs and reflect humane values.

In practice, this might mean that AI generates hundreds of potential layouts for a social media platform, each optimized for different metrics: engagement, user well-being, information quality, or community building. The human designer then evaluates these options not just for their technical merit but for their social implications. Which designs encourage meaningful connections versus shallow interactions? Which support diverse voices versus amplifying dominant perspectives? Which promote healthy usage patterns versus addictive behaviors? The collaboration extends beyond individual projects to influence the broader evolution of design practice. AI tools are democratizing certain aspects of design, making sophisticated analysis and rapid prototyping available to teams that previously lacked such resources. Small nonprofits can now create interfaces that rival those of major corporations. Educational institutions can provide students with design capabilities that were once available only in professional studios.

Yet this democratization also increases the importance of human judgment and ethical reasoning. As design tools become more powerful and accessible, the responsibility for using them wisely becomes more distributed and more critical. Every designer working with AI becomes a steward of its capabilities, responsible for ensuring that increased power leads to increased benefit rather than harm.

Guardrails for Responsible AI

If AI is to stand beside us as a co-designer, it must be a responsible one. The power to shape digital experiences carries profound ethical obligations, and these obligations become more complex when we share design authority with systems that lack human moral intuition. Without careful guidance and robust safeguards, AI risks amplifying existing biases, overlooking the needs of marginalized communities, and perpetuating systemic injustices at an unprecedented scale.

The early years of AI deployment in design have already revealed these dangers with troubling clarity. Facial recognition systems have exhibited racial bias, misclassified faces and leading to wrongful arrests. Recommendation algorithms have created filter bubbles that polarize communities and spread disinformation. Automated hiring tools have discriminated against women and minorities. Social media algorithms optimized for engagement have contributed to mental health crises among young people. These failures occurred not because the AI systems were malicious but because they reflected the biases present in their training data and optimization targets. AI learns from human-generated examples, and those examples inevitably contain the prejudices, oversights, and blind spots of their creators. When these biases are amplified by AI's scale and speed, they can cause harm far beyond what their human counterparts might have achieved.

To ensure that AI serves as a responsible co-designer, three fundamental commitments are essential:

Transparency and Explainability

AI must not operate as a black box, generating solutions through inscrutable processes that resist human understanding. Instead, it must function as an explainable collaborator, capable of articulating its reasoning and making its decision-making process visible to human partners.

This transparency serves multiple purposes. First, it enables designers to understand and evaluate AI suggestions, distinguishing between proposals based on solid evidence and those reflecting spurious correlations. When an AI suggests a particular color scheme for improved accessibility, designers need to understand whether this recommendation stems from rigorous usability research or from biased training data that overlooked certain user populations. Second, transparency enables continuous learning and improvement. When humans can understand how AI reaches its conclusions, they can provide more targeted feedback, helping the system refine its understanding and avoid future errors. This creates a virtuous cycle where human expertise, and AI capabilities mutually reinforce each other. Third, transparency supports accountability. When AI-assisted designs cause problems, teams need to understand how those problems arose and how to prevent them in the future. Opaque AI systems make such learning impossible, turning failures into mysteries rather than opportunities for growth. Achieving this transparency requires both technical and organizational changes. AI systems must be designed with interpretability as a primary goal, not an afterthought. Design teams must develop new skills for working with AI explanations, learning to interpret confidence levels, identify potential biases, and translate AI insights into human-understandable terms.

Human Accountability and Override Authority

While AI can suggest and optimize, humans must retain ultimate responsibility for design decisions and their consequences. This principle goes beyond mere lip service; it requires establishing clear chains of accountability and ensuring that human designers have both the authority and the capability to override AI recommendations when necessary. Human accountability means that every AI-generated design element must be consciously approved by a human who understands its implications. It means establishing review processes that examine not just whether designs work but whether they work ethically. It means training designers to recognize when AI suggestions might have unintended consequences and empowering them to reject recommendations that conflict with human values.

This accountability extends to the development and deployment of AI design tools themselves. Organizations using AI in design must take responsibility for understanding how their systems work, what biases they might contain, and what safeguards are necessary to prevent harm. They must invest in ongoing monitoring, establishing feedback mechanisms that can detect problems quickly and respond appropriately.

The challenge lies in maintaining meaningful human control while leveraging AI's capabilities effectively. Too much intervention stifles AI's potential contributions; too little risks abdication of human responsibility. The solution requires developing new frameworks for human-AI collaboration that preserve human agency while embracing machine intelligence.

Inclusivity and Representative Data

AI systems learn from the data they are trained on, making the composition of training datasets a critical factor in determining whether AI serves all users equitably. If training data primarily represents certain demographics, languages, or cultural contexts, the resulting AI will excel at serving those groups while potentially failing or even harming others. Ensuring inclusivity requires deliberate effort to collect diverse, representative datasets that reflect the full spectrum of human experience. This means including voices from different geographic regions, cultural backgrounds, economic circumstances, ages, abilities, and technological contexts. It means recognizing that "default" users are often assumed to be young, affluent, technically sophisticated, and from dominant cultural groups and actively working to include perspectives that challenge these assumptions. But inclusivity goes beyond data collection to encompass the entire AI development process. The teams building AI design tools must themselves be diverse, bringing different perspectives to bear on questions of what problems matter, how solutions should be evaluated, and what constitutes success. Homogeneous teams, no matter how well-intentioned, inevitably create blind spots that can lead to exclusionary designs.

Inclusivity also requires ongoing vigilance. As AI systems are deployed and used, they must be continuously monitored for bias and discrimination. This monitoring should include both quantitative analyses measuring outcomes across different user groups and qualitative feedback from diverse communities about their experiences with AI-designed systems.

The Ethics of Augmentation

Beyond these foundational requirements lies a deeper philosophical question: What does it mean to augment human creativity responsibly? As AI becomes more sophisticated, the line between human and machine contributions to design may become increasingly blurred. This blurring raises questions about authorship, authenticity, and the nature of creative work itself. Some worry that reliance on AI might diminish human creative capacity, creating a generation of designers who can curate and refine AI suggestions but lack the skills to generate original ideas independently. Others argue that this concern misunderstands the nature of creativity, which has always involved building upon existing ideas, tools, and techniques. The responsible path forward likely involves maintaining a balance using AI to extend human capabilities without replacing human agency. This might mean ensuring that designers continue to develop core creative skills even as they learn to collaborate with AI. It might mean establishing educational programs that teach both technical AI literacy and the humanistic skills that remain uniquely valuable.

The New Design Process

The integration of AI as a co-designer is reshaping not just the tools we use but the fundamental processes through which design unfolds. Traditional design methodologies, developed for human-only teams, are evolving to accommodate the unique capabilities and limitations of artificial intelligence partners.

Iterative Ideation at Scale

In traditional design, ideation phases often involved structured brainstorming sessions where human teams generated ideas through discussion, sketching, and collaborative exercises. While valuable, these approaches were inherently limited by human cognitive constraints, the number of ideas a team could generate, evaluate, and develop within practical time limits.

AI collaboration transforms ideation into a process of iterative exploration at an unprecedented scale. Designers can now begin with broad directional input, "design a dashboard for renewable energy monitoring," and receive dozens of initial concepts within minutes. Each concept can serve as a starting point for deeper exploration, with AI generating variations that explore different aspects of the challenge. This process resembles biological evolution more than traditional engineering. Ideas multiply, mutate, and combine in unexpected ways. Promising concepts survive and reproduce, while less successful approaches fade away. The designer's role shifts from generating all ideas personally to guiding this evolutionary process, selecting characteristics that serve human needs and values.

The speed and scale of AI-assisted ideation enable exploration of design spaces that were previously inaccessible. Designers can pursue multiple radically different approaches simultaneously, comparing solutions that optimize different user goals or technical constraints. This parallel exploration often reveals insights that sequential design processes might miss discovering, for instance, that an interface optimized for speed naturally becomes more accessible to users with motor impairments.

Predictive User Experience Modeling

One of AI's most powerful contributions to design lies in its ability to model and predict user behavior with unprecedented sophistication. Traditional user experience research relied on surveys, interviews, focus groups, and usability testing, valuable methods that nonetheless provided limited samples of user behavior under artificial conditions.

AI can analyze behavioral data from thousands or millions of real users, identifying patterns that reveal how people actually interact with digital systems in their natural environments. It can predict how interface changes might affect user satisfaction, task completion rates, accessibility, and long-term engagement. This predictive capability enables designers to evaluate options before implementation, reducing the risk of costly mistakes and improving outcomes for users. More importantly, AI can model the behavior of diverse user populations, helping designers understand how their choices might affect different groups differently. It can reveal that an interface change that improves efficiency for experienced users might create barriers for newcomers, or that a design optimized for smartphone users might be problematic for people using assistive technologies. This predictive modeling extends beyond individual interfaces to encompass entire user journeys. AI can simulate how users might move through complex systems over time, identifying potential points of confusion, frustration, or abandonment. It can model how different design decisions might affect user trust, satisfaction, and long-term relationships with a product or service.

Real-Time Adaptive Design

Perhaps the most revolutionary aspect of AI co-design is its potential to create systems that adapt to users in real-time, continuously optimizing themselves based on actual usage patterns and individual needs. Rather than designing static interfaces that attempt to serve all users identically, AI enables the creation of responsive systems that learn and evolve.

This adaptive capability represents a fundamental shift from designing products to designing design processes, creating systems that can redesign themselves in response to new information and changing circumstances. An AI-assisted interface might notice that certain users consistently struggle with particular interactions and automatically offer alternative approaches. It might detect patterns of user stress or confusion and adjust its behavior to provide additional support. The implications extend far beyond user interface optimization. Adaptive AI systems can help address the persistent challenge of designing for global audiences with diverse needs, preferences, and cultural contexts. Rather than creating one-size-fits-all solutions or maintaining expensive localized versions, AI can enable single systems that gracefully adapt to different cultural, linguistic, and contextual requirements.

Collaboration, Not Replacement

The fear that AI will replace human designers reflects anxiety about technological unemployment but misses the deeper truth about what design accomplishes. True design is more than solving functional problems; it is about asking the right questions, understanding unspoken needs, and embedding meaning, dignity, and human values into systems that will shape how people experience the world. AI's remarkable pattern-matching abilities and computational power make it excellent at optimizing for measurable outcomes: reducing loading times, increasing click-through rates, minimizing user errors, or maximizing engagement. These are valuable contributions, but they represent only the most quantifiable aspects of good design. The qualitative dimensions of beauty, meaning, emotional resonance, cultural appropriateness, and ethical soundness require human judgment, empathy, and wisdom. Consider the design of educational software for children. AI might analyze thousands of successful educational apps and identify interaction patterns that correlate with improved learning outcomes. It might propose game mechanics that increase engagement, visual designs that enhance focus, and progression systems that maintain motivation. These suggestions could be technically sound and statistically validated.

Yet a human designer must grapple with questions that transcend optimization: Does this interface respect children's developmental needs or manipulate their psychology for engagement? Does it encourage creativity and independent thinking or reward conformity and passive consumption? Does it support diverse learning styles and cultural backgrounds or impose narrow definitions of success? These questions require not just data analysis but moral reasoning, cultural sensitivity, and a deep understanding of human development.

The collaboration works best when both parties understand and embrace their complementary roles. AI becomes a powerful research assistant, pattern detector, and option generator capable of rapidly exploring design spaces that would take human team months to investigate thoroughly. It can identify best practices from across industries, suggest novel combinations of existing elements, and predict the likely outcomes of different design decisions.

Humans become curators, interpreters, and ethical guardians, ensuring that AI's suggestions serve authentic human needs rather than abstract optimization metrics. They provide the context, values, and judgment that transform efficient solutions into meaningful experiences. They ask the questions that matter most: not just "does this work?" but "should this exist?" and "what kind of world are we creating?" This division of labor leverages the unique strengths of both human and artificial intelligence while mitigating their respective limitations. AI struggles with context, meaning, and values but excels at scale, pattern recognition, and optimization. Humans sometimes miss subtle patterns or fail to consider all possibilities but excel at understanding purpose, emotion, and ethical implications.

The result is a design that possesses both computational power and human wisdom, systems that perform efficiently while serving humane goals. Neither humans nor AI could achieve these outcomes independently, but together they can create digital experiences that are simultaneously sophisticated and soulful.

Case Studies in Human-AI Design Collaboration

Accessibility-First Web Design

A nonprofit organization working on digital inclusion partnered with AI to redesign its website for maximum accessibility. The AI analyzed accessibility guidelines and user behavior data from assistive technology users, and successful accessible designs from across the web. It generated interface concepts that are optimized for screen reader navigation, keyboard-only interaction, and various visual impairments. The human design team brought crucial context that no dataset could provide understanding of the stigma often associated with disability services, recognition that accessibility features benefit all users (not just those with diagnosed impairments), and insight into the emotional experience of seeking support. They guided the AI toward solutions that felt welcoming rather than clinical, empowering rather than patronizing.

The final design exceeded traditional accessibility compliance while feeling natural and inviting to all users. Features designed for screen readers improved the experience for people using mobile devices in bright sunlight. Navigation optimized for motor impairments proved more efficient for everyone. The AI's analytical capabilities, combined with human empathy, created a truly universal design.

Cultural Adaptation of Global Software

A technology company needed to adapt its productivity software for markets across six continents, each with distinct cultural norms around hierarchy, communication, and workflow. Traditional localization approaches focused primarily on language translation and basic cultural customization, often missing subtle but important cultural differences in user expectations and interaction patterns. AI analysis of user behavior data across different regions revealed patterns that human researchers might have missed: differences in how teams from various cultures approached collaborative tasks, varying preferences for direct versus indirect communication interfaces, and distinct expectations about privacy and data sharing. Human cultural experts interpreted these patterns, explaining their deeper significance and helping the AI understand the values and assumptions underlying different behavioral patterns. They ensured that adaptations respected cultural differences without reinforcing stereotypes, and they identified areas where cross-cultural exchange might actually benefit all users. The resulting software featured intelligent cultural adaptation that went far beyond language translation. Interface elements, workflow structures, and communication features adjusted to match local cultural expectations while maintaining core functionality. Users in each region felt that the software understood and respected their way of working.

Emotional Design for Mental Health Applications

A team developing a mental health app faced the complex challenge of creating interfaces that could support people during emotional crises while avoiding the risk of inadvertent harm. Traditional user research in this domain is particularly challenging, as users experiencing mental health difficulties may not be able to articulate their needs clearly, and ethical constraints limit the types of research that can be conducted.

AI provided analytical capabilities that supplemented traditional research methods. It analyzed anonymous usage patterns from existing mental health apps, identifying interface elements and interaction patterns that correlated with positive outcomes. It modeled how different design choices might affect user stress levels, engagement, and help-seeking behavior.

Human designers and mental health professionals provided essential guidance about the emotional and therapeutic dimensions that data alone couldn't capture. They helped the AI understand the difference between engagement and genuine support, between efficiency and healing. They ensured that optimizations for user retention didn't exploit vulnerable mental states and that features designed to provide help actually empowered users rather than creating dependence. The collaboration produced an app that balanced AI's optimization capabilities with human understanding of trauma, recovery, and resilience. Features adapted to users' emotional states while respecting their autonomy. The interface provided efficient access to resources while maintaining the warmth and empathy essential for therapeutic relationships.

Challenges and Limitations

Despite its promise, human-AI collaboration in design faces significant challenges that must be acknowledged and addressed. Understanding these limitations is essential for realistic expectations and responsible implementation.

As AI becomes more sophisticated in generating design ideas, questions of authorship and credit become increasingly complex. When a breakthrough design emerges from human-AI collaboration, how do we fairly attribute credit? This question matters not just for intellectual property but for understanding the creative process itself and ensuring that both human and AI contributions are appropriately recognized and rewarded. Traditional notions of authorship assume individual human creativity. Legal and professional frameworks for recognizing design achievements may need fundamental revision to accommodate collaborative relationships that include artificial intelligence. This challenge extends beyond design to encompass all creative fields where AI plays an increasing role.

Over-Reliance and Skill Atrophy

There is a legitimate concern that excessive dependence on AI might lead to atrophy of fundamental design skills. If designers become too reliant on AI for ideation, analysis, and optimization, they might lose the ability to think independently about design challenges. This risk is particularly acute for emerging designers who might learn to curate AI suggestions rather than develop their own creative capabilities. Addressing this challenge requires thoughtful education and practice. Design programs must evolve to teach both AI collaboration skills and fundamental creative abilities. Professional development should emphasize the complementary nature of human-AI partnerships rather than positioning AI as a replacement for human creativity.

Bias Amplification and Homogenization

While AI can process diverse inputs, it might also amplify existing biases or push designs toward homogenization. If most successful designs in training data reflect certain cultural assumptions or aesthetic preferences, AI might perpetuate these patterns rather than encouraging innovation or diversity. This risk requires active countermeasures: diverse training data, bias detection tools, and human oversight specifically focused on identifying and addressing discriminatory patterns. Design teams must remain vigilant about the assumptions embedded in their AI tools and work actively to counteract tendencies toward bias or homogenization.

10. Preparing for Collaborative Futures

The transition to AI-assisted design requires new skills, new tools, and new ways of thinking about creative work. Design education must evolve to prepare students for collaboration with artificial intelligence while preserving the uniquely human capabilities that will remain essential. Designers working with AI need to develop hybrid competencies that blend traditional design skills with AI literacy. This includes understanding how AI systems work (without necessarily mastering their technical implementation), learning to provide effective feedback to AI systems, developing skills for evaluating AI-generated suggestions, and maintaining awareness of AI limitations and biases. These skills extend beyond technical knowledge to encompass new forms of creative leadership. AI collaboration requires designers to be more explicit about their values, goals, and constraints. It requires skills for facilitating human-AI teamwork, much as traditional design requires skills for facilitating human collaboration.

Evolving Design Tools

The software tools used for design are rapidly evolving to incorporate AI capabilities. Future design environments will likely feel less like traditional software applications and more like collaborative workspaces where human designers work alongside AI partners. These tools must be designed to support effective collaboration while maintaining human agency and creative control. The best AI-assisted design tools will make the collaboration feel natural and intuitive rather than mechanical or impersonal. They will provide transparency about AI reasoning while avoiding overwhelming designers with technical details. They will enable rapid iteration and exploration while maintaining coherent design narratives and consistent user experiences.

Institutional Changes

Organizations employing AI in design must develop new policies, procedures, and ethical frameworks to guide this collaboration responsibly. This includes establishing clear guidelines for when and how AI should be used, creating review processes for AI-assisted designs, and developing criteria for evaluating the success of human-AI collaborations. Professional design organizations, educational institutions, and industry groups must work together to establish best practices, ethical standards, and educational curricula that prepare designers for collaborative futures. This coordination will help ensure that AI's integration into design practice enhances rather than diminishes the profession's capacity to serve human needs.

The dawn of AI as co-designer represents one of the most significant shifts in creative practice since the invention of digital tools themselves. This transformation is not the end of human creativity but its dramatic expansion, an invitation to explore design possibilities that were previously beyond our reach while ensuring that human values and wisdom guide every step of the journey. Machines now imagine, explore, and propose alongside us, bringing computational power and pattern recognition that complement human intuition and moral reasoning. Their role is not to replace human designers but to amplify human capabilities, to serve as tireless research partners and creative catalysts that help us discover solutions we might never have found alone.

Yet with this power comes profound responsibility. As we invite AI into the creative process, we must remain vigilant guardians of human dignity, equity, and flourishing. We must ensure that our artificial collaborators serve authentic human needs rather than abstract optimization metrics. We must maintain human agency while embracing machine intelligence, preserving the values and wisdom that make design a fundamentally humanistic practice. The future of software will not be written by humans alone, nor by AI alone, but by partnerships that honor the unique strengths of both. In this collaboration, we have the opportunity to create digital systems that are simultaneously more efficient and more humane, more powerful and more ethical, and more innovative and more inclusive than anything either humans or machines could produce independently.

This partnership requires courage the courage to embrace new ways of working while holding fast to timeless values. It requires wisdom the wisdom to know when to trust AI suggestions and when to follow human intuition. Most of all, it requires humility and recognition that this collaboration is still in its earliest stages and that its full potential remains to be discovered.

The story of design continues, enriched by new voices and new possibilities. The future of software will not be written alone. It will be written together, in dialogue between humans. creativity and artificial intelligence, guided by a shared commitment to creating technology that serves the flourishing of all humanity. In accepting AI as our co-designer, we embark on perhaps the most profound creative dialogue in human history, one that has the potential to reshape not just our digital tools but our understanding of creativity itself. The responsibility is immense, the possibilities boundless, and the future entirely in our collective hands.

Chapter 5

Ethics Woven into Architecture

In an era defined by rapid technological advancement, the digital landscape is undergoing a profound transformation. We are moving beyond the simple creation of tools to the construction of a new kind of world a world built on code. This new reality, as the provided text powerfully argues, requires a fundamental shift in our approach to design. The principles of **ethics woven into architecture** are no longer abstract philosophical considerations but essential, practical requirements for building a future that is just, equitable, and sustainable. This is a call to action for every creator, designer, and developer to recognize that their work is not neutral; it is an act of ethical significance that shapes society as profoundly as any physical structure.

The Foundation of Intentional Design: A Moral Blueprint

The notion that every line of code carries an ethical weight is a radical but necessary reframing of the software development process. We often think of code in terms of its functionality, does it work? Is it fast? Is it secure? These are crucial questions, but they overlook the more subtle, yet more consequential, ethical dimensions. The article rightly points out that these dimensions are often buried in defaults and assumptions, forming a "moral blueprint" that dictates the system's underlying values.

Consider a seemingly innocuous design choice: a user interface that defaults to English. On the surface, this might seem like a practical decision for a U.S.-based company, but it invisibly excludes billions of people who don't speak the language. This isn't just a usability issue; it's an ethical one. It sends a message that certain users are "normal," while others are an afterthought. Similarly, an algorithm that prioritizes "engagement" above all else, without considering the potential for psychological harm or the spread of misinformation, is making an ethical choice to favor profit over user well-being. The consequences of such choices are no longer contained within a single application; they can influence how millions of people perceive truth, interact with each other, and even engage in democratic processes.

The history of software is replete with examples of what happens when this moral blueprint is not intentional. Social media platforms, in their pursuit of virality, created echo chambers and amplified extreme viewpoints, contributing to social polarization. Predictive policing systems, built on historical data that reflect existing racial biases, perpetuated cycles of injustice rather than preventing crime. These were not technical failures; they were ethical failures of **architecture**. The systems were working as designed, but the design itself was flawed from an ethical standpoint. It was optimized for one set of values (e.g., engagement, efficiency) while neglecting others (e.g., inclusivity, justice).

Moving forward, the first step in ethical architecture is to make this moral blueprint explicit. Designers must move beyond asking, "Can we build this?" and instead ask, "Should we build this, and what values will it embed?" This requires a deliberate process of ethical foresight, where potential harms and biases are identified and mitigated from the very beginning. This includes considering who the system might exclude, what unintended consequences it might have, and how it might be misused. The moral blueprint must be a living document, integrated into the design and development process, rather than a checklist to be completed at the end. By making our values explicit, we can build systems that don't just work but that work for everyone, fostering justice rather than amplifying harm.

The Pillar of Clarity: Transparency as a Foundational Design Principle

As digital systems grow in complexity, their inner workings often become opaque, a phenomenon the text aptly describes as the "black box." This is especially true for systems powered by artificial intelligence, where even the creators may not fully understand why a particular output was generated. This lack of clarity is not merely a technical inconvenience; it is a profound ethical problem that erodes trust and disempowers users. When a system makes a decision that affects a person's life say, a loan application, a medical diagnosis, or a criminal justice recommendation, the inability to understand how that decision was reached is an affront to human dignity.

Therefore, **transparency must become a foundational design principle**, not just a feature to be added if time and budget allow. The goal is not to expose every line of code or overwhelm users with technical jargon. Instead, the focus should be on providing a clear and understandable explanation for a system's actions. This can be achieved by designing systems that are inherently explainable. For example, a credit score application might not only provide the final score but also explain the factors that contributed to it, such as payment history and credit utilization. An AI-powered medical platform could explain its diagnostic recommendation by referencing specific data points from the patient's history and relevant medical literature. This approach transforms the user's relationship with the technology from one of passive acceptance to one of informed partnership.

Transparency also serves as a critical tool for accountability. When a system is transparent, its logic can be audited, questioned, and contested. This is crucial for both users and regulators. If a system's decisions are opaque, it becomes impossible to identify and rectify biases or errors. This is particularly important in high-stakes domains like healthcare, finance, and criminal justice, where a system's flawed logic can have devastating consequences. A transparent system allows for collective scrutiny, which in turn fosters trust and ensures that the system serves the public good.

Imagine the healthcare platform described in the text: an AI recommendation for a treatment is not just presented as a final verdict but as a conclusion supported by specific evidence. This level of clarity is not just about compliance; it is about building a foundation of trust that can endure for generations. When people understand why a system is making a particular recommendation, they are more likely to accept it, and they are also empowered to challenge it if it seems incorrect. This kind of transparency creates a feedback loop that allows the system to be continuously improved and refined, ensuring that it remains fair, accurate, and ethical over time.

The System of Responsibility: Accountability in Every Layer

Ethics, as the article emphasizes, cannot be a separate department or a policy document that sits on a shelf. It must be woven into every layer of the software architecture from the user interface to the database, from the development workflow to the deployment strategy. This is the principle of accountability in every layer. This means that when harm occurs, responsibility can be traced and addressed, preventing the "responsibility gaps" that are all too common in complex digital systems.

The diffusion of blame is a serious ethical problem in modern software. When a system's flawed output harms a user, it can be difficult to determine who is at fault. Was it the developer who wrote the code? The product manager who set the requirements? The data scientist who used a biased dataset? Or the executive who prioritized speed over safety? To prevent this, future software must be designed with explicit mechanisms for accountability.

One such mechanism is auditability. Systems must be built to be reviewed and inspected over time. This means not only logging actions but also documenting the reasoning behind key design decisions. Just as a building's blueprints are preserved for future generations, a software system's ethical blueprint should be a permanent record. This allows future developers to understand not just what a system does, but why it was built the way it was.

This is essential for ongoing maintenance, security, and ethical stewardship.

Another crucial component is the establishment of ethical checkpoints in the development process. These are specific decision points where the potential impact of a feature or a design choice is consciously evaluated. This moves ethical considerations from a post-hoc analysis to a proactive part of the development lifecycle. This could involve a team-wide discussion about a new feature's potential for misuse or a formal review of the datasets used in a machine learning model to ensure they are not biased.

Finally, there is the principle of shared responsibility. In modern development, where teams are often cross-functional, accountability for a system's outcomes should be collective, not individual. This means that a team, not just a single coder or executive, is responsible for the ethical implications of their work. This fosters a culture of stewardship, where every member of the team feels a sense of ownership over the system's impact on the world. It reframes accountability not as a punishment but as an act of care, a recognition that the systems we build affect lives and therefore deserve to be crafted with integrity and watched over with vigilance.

The true legacy of software will not be its technical features or its market performance. It will be the values it embeds and the trust it builds. By weaving ethics into the very foundation of our digital architecture through moral blueprints, transparency, and accountability, we are not just building efficient code. We are building enduring structures of trust that will shape the lives of generations yet to come. This is the profound and necessary challenge of our time: to design with not only convenience in mind but also with a profound and unwavering conscience.

Chapter 6

Global Collaboration and Shared Codebases

In an era of unprecedented digital integration, the very fabric of human civilization is being rewoven. While our ancestors built great cathedrals of stone and vast networks of roads to connect their empires, we are now constructing a new kind of global infrastructure: shared codebases. These are not merely technical repositories; they are living ecosystems of human collaboration, where a line of code written in one corner of the world can instantly become a building block for innovation in another. The original text correctly identifies that this new paradigm represents a fundamental shift in how humanity creates and progresses. It is a model where borders blur, ownership becomes fluid, and the speed of advancement is dictated by our ability to collaborate. Yet, this remarkable interconnectedness is not without its profound challenges. To build a digital future that is not only functional but also just and sustainable, we must address the complex human, social, and ethical dimensions that underlie this shared digital enterprise. This requires us to look beyond the elegant algorithms and technical architectures to see the human ecosystem that makes it all possible.

The Commons of Code as a Cultural Monument

The shared codebases that power so much of modern life, from operating systems like Linux to vast machine learning frameworks like TensorFlow, are the modern-day equivalent of a public common. They are vast, open spaces where individuals and organizations from every corner of the globe contribute their time, skill, and creative energy. Unlike proprietary software, where the source code is a closely guarded secret and progress is directed by a single company, open-source projects are a testament to the power of collective intelligence. They are not the work of a single genius but are, as the text suggests, like cathedrals-built stone by stone by thousands of dedicated contributors over years and decades. This collaborative model embodies a profound and beautiful paradox: a shared codebase is at once deeply fragile and remarkably resilient.

Its fragility stems from the very nature of its decentralized, often voluntary, structure. A core group of maintainers, sometimes just a handful of individuals, bears the immense and often uncompensated burden of governance, security, and the sheer volume of updates. This can lead to a precarious situation known as the "bus factor", a measure of the number of people who, if hit by a bus, would cause a project to fail. The burnout of a key maintainer or the loss of interest from a small team can put a widely used and critical piece of digital infrastructure at risk. Many open-source projects, particularly those that are not backed by large corporations, struggle with chronic underfunding and the immense pressure placed on volunteers. This is a vulnerability that echoes the neglect of public infrastructure in the physical world, where a crumbling bridge or a forgotten public library signals a societal failure to maintain shared resources.

And yet, within this fragility lies a remarkable resilience. Because the code is open and accessible to all, the knowledge is never truly lost. If a project falters, anyone can "fork" it, creating a new branch of development that can repair, expand, and sustain the original idea. The wisdom of the crowd acts as a powerful corrective force. A bug identified by a developer in Tokyo can be fixed by a student in Buenos Aires within hours. This distributed, global network of contributors ensures that the system can adapt and self-correct far more rapidly than any centralized, top-down structure. The long tail of contributors, those who make a single, small change or file an obscure bug report, are just as vital to the ecosystem's health as the core maintainers. They are the silent caretakers of the digital commons, ensuring their longevity and utility.

Ultimately, shared codebases are not just technical artifacts; they are deeply significant **cultural monuments**. They embody a shared recognition that some knowledge and some tools are too important to be monopolized. They represent a philosophical commitment to freedom and accessibility, a belief that the most valuable and fundamental building blocks of our digital future should be unencumbered by profit motives and available to all. Designing for future generations means, above all else, protecting and nurturing this ethos. This requires us to build infrastructure that not only supports the code itself but also sustains the community that creates it, ensuring that contributors are valued, their work is recognized, and the spirit of collective ownership is not eroded by commercial pressures or institutional neglect.

The Human Fabric of Global Collaboration

The true transformative power of shared codebases lies in their ability to facilitate collaboration across borders. A developer in a small village in Nigeria solving a local problem with a custom application might create a function that, when contributed to a public repository, provides a key piece of a solution for a global healthcare system. A high school student in a developing nation, with access to a computer and the internet, can contribute to a complex machine learning library, indirectly empowering researchers at world-renowned institutions. Every line of code, every pull request, and every bug report is a thread that weaves together a global fabric of progress. The digital world offers a level playing field where a brilliant idea from anywhere can have an impact everywhere.

However, the path to true collaboration is not as simple as granting access to the internet. Significant obstacles, often invisible to those in privileged positions, continue to shape and limit participation. Language barriers are a primary hurdle. While English has become the de facto language of programming, this excludes countless brilliant minds who may not be fluent. Documentation, tutorials, and project discussions are often solely in English, creating a steep learning curve and a sense of alienation for non-native speakers. Cultural differences in communication styles can also lead to misunderstandings, with a direct critique from one culture being perceived as a personal attack in another. This requires a new level of empathy and cross-cultural literacy within the open-source community.

Even more pervasive is the issue of infrastructure and access. A developer in a region with unstable internet or frequent power outages simply cannot engage in the same way as someone with high-speed, always-on connectivity. They cannot easily clone multi-gigabyte repositories, participate in real-time video calls with a globally distributed team, or quickly test and deploy changes. This creates a digital divide that is not only about access to technology but about the ability to participate in the collaborative process itself. The result is that the loudest and most influential voices in these global projects often come from privileged contexts, those with stable infrastructure, institutional support, and a high degree of digital literacy. The solutions, therefore, must be architectural and inclusive by design. This includes creating low-bandwidth tools, supporting asynchronous communication, and prioritizing multilingual documentation and communities.

Designing for inclusivity also means creating governance models that explicitly value and seek out voices from the margins. This requires a conscious effort to challenge the status quo and to recognize that innovation is a collective endeavor, not a top-down one. Mentorship programs, dedicated funding for contributors from underrepresented regions, and a commitment to equitable decision-making are all part of building a truly global and representative commons. The measure of our success will not be the number of contributions we receive but the diversity of the people making them. We must ask ourselves at every step of the design process: Who is being excluded by default? Who is struggling to participate? And how can we re-engineer our systems to create a space where every human being, regardless of their background, can contribute their unique genius to the collective good?

The Ethical Imperative of Stewardship

Shared codebases are not merely about the present moment; they are blueprints for the future. The code we write and the systems we design today will form the foundation for the applications, tools, and technologies of tomorrow. This is our inheritance, and with it comes a profound responsibility to act as good stewards. Stewardship is a more encompassing concept than simple maintenance. It is a conscious, ethical act of responsibility that requires us to build with the next generation in mind.

One of the most critical aspects of this stewardship is documentation. We must move beyond the perfunctory documentation of APIs and functions. True stewardship demands that we document not only what a system does, but why it was designed that way. This involves creating "architectural decision records" that explain the ethical, technical, and historical context of a given choice. Such documentation serves as a guide for future developers, preventing them from repeating the mistakes of the past and providing them with a historical record of our collective journey. It transforms the act of documentation from a mundane chore into a vital act of caring for those who will inherit our work.

Furthermore, stewardship requires architectural foresight. We must design systems that are not monolithic and brittle but modular, adaptable, and open to reinterpretation. Just as Roman engineers-built roads that outlasted their empire, our digital architects must build frameworks that can evolve with changing technologies and ethical standards. This means building systems with clear separation of concerns, well-defined interfaces, and a commitment to open standards. A poorly designed, tightly coupled system becomes a burden, a "legacy" that future generations are forced to either maintain at great cost or completely rewrite. A well-designed, modular system, however, can be continuously extended and improved upon, ensuring its longevity and relevance.

Finally, stewardship requires institutional imagination. We cannot rely solely on the goodwill of volunteers to maintain and govern these critical pieces of digital infrastructure. Just as governments and institutions fund the construction and maintenance of physical roads, bridges, and libraries, they must also recognize that open, shared code is a form of public infrastructure that requires sustained financial and institutional support. Universities should integrate open-source ethics into their computer science curricula, and governments should create funding models that support the work of maintainers. When we neglect this responsibility, we are not just failing a few open-source projects; we are gambling with the digital inheritance of all of humanity.

In conclusion, the cathedrals of our digital age are the shared codebases that we are building together. They are a testament to what humanity can achieve when we transcend borders and allow our collective imagination to converge. But they also present a profound challenge. We are called upon to build not just for today's innovation but for tomorrow's inheritance. By consciously weaving in principles of inclusivity, governance, and stewardship, we ensure that the legacy we leave behind is not one of decay and neglect, but one of resilience, justice, and enduring trust. The greatest legacy of this era will not be the speed of our code but the depth of our conscience in creating it.

Chapter 7

Ethics in Code The Moral Compass of Tomorrow's Software

Software is not just technical, it is moral. Every interface nudge behavior, every algorithm filter perception, every infrastructure embeds decisions about who is included and who is excluded. To pretend otherwise is to ignore the reality that code shapes lives. Unlike a hammer or a pen, which are tools of individual use, software today operates at planetary scale, influencing billions simultaneously. The ethical consequences of software are no longer hypothetical; they are woven into the fabric of daily existence.

To design software for generations ahead, ethics cannot be a decorative addition or a "compliance box" to tick. It must be the foundation. Just as an architect would never design a bridge without considering safety, engineers cannot design digital infrastructures without considering justice, fairness, transparency, and responsibility.

This chapter explores ethics in code not as an abstract philosophy but as a lived, practical discipline. It asks us to see algorithms as carriers of values, to recognize the immense responsibility of scale, and to design systems with foresight and care. Ultimately, it argues that to code ethically is to contribute not merely to technology, but to humanity's collective blueprint for tomorrow.

1. Algorithms as Value Carriers

For decades, engineers and computer scientists described algorithms as "neutral", mathematical recipes for processing data. But neutrality is an illusion. Algorithms do not exist in a vacuum; they are created by people, trained on data reflecting human histories, and deployed in contexts shaped by power and inequality.

Take, for instance, predictive policing systems. At first glance, they seem like impartial tools: algorithms designed to identify where crimes are likely to occur. But because they are trained on historical crime data, data that itself reflects decades of over-policing in marginalized neighborhoods, the system "predicts" that those same neighborhoods are more crime prone. The cycle continues: more patrols, more arrests, more "evidence" that the algorithm was correct. What appears neutral is, in fact, an automated echo of bias.

Or consider hiring algorithms. Some corporations sought to automate resume screening to eliminate human prejudice. Yet many such systems ended up replicating discriminatory patterns, favoring male candidates or applicants from elite institutions, because the training data reflected the biases of past hiring decisions. Far from eliminating prejudice, the system baked it in at scale.

Recommendation engines are another vivid example. Optimized for "engagement," they push content that captures attention, often sensational, polarizing, or misleading. Platforms like YouTube and Facebook have been criticized for radicalizing users, not because anyone explicitly programmed them to promote extremism, but because the system's underlying value, maximizing time spent on site, rewarded outrage over nuance.

These examples underscore a key truth: algorithms are value carriers. They embody choices about what matters: efficiency versus fairness, speed versus transparency, profitability versus safety. They encode worldviews about what is worth optimizing and what is expendable. Even decisions about what data to collect, what categories to define, and what outputs to prioritize are moral choices disguised as technical parameters.

Recognizing algorithms as value carriers shifts how we approach design. It requires us to ask: Whose values are being carried? Who benefits? Who bears the cost? This recognition does not paralyze innovation, it enriches it. It transforms engineering from narrow technical execution into a broader practice of responsibility.

Future generations will inherit not just our systems but also the values we encode within them. If we fail to acknowledge this, they will inherit biases fossilized in algorithms, amplified by scale, and resistant to reform. But if we embrace our role as ethical architects, we can leave behind systems that carry values of fairness, inclusivity, and care, values worth transmitting across time.

2. Responsibility in the Age of Scale

In the analog world, flaws were often local. A poorly built bridge endangered one community, but not the world. In the digital era, however, scale changes everything. A single miscalculation can ripple across nations. A bug in a global payment system can halt economies. A security vulnerability in widely used libraries can expose billions of devices.

This scale transforms responsibility. Engineers today wield a kind of influence unprecedented in human history. A developer adjusting a recommendation algorithm may inadvertently affect political discourse across continents. A design choice in a messaging app may alter how families communicate, how activists organize, or how misinformation spreads. What feels like a small tweak in a sprint cycle may reshape culture at scale.

Consider the case of social media. What began as a way to connect friends evolved into platforms that shape elections, mental health, and even geopolitical stability. The engineers who designed "like" buttons and infinite scroll likely did not anticipate that these features would fuel addictive behavior, distort public discourse, and contribute to mental health crises among youth. Yet scale magnified their effects in ways no one could ignore.

Or think of financial algorithms. In 2010, the "Flash Crash" wiped nearly a trillion dollars in market value within minutes due to high-frequency trading algorithms interacting in unpredictable ways. What might have been a local glitch in another era became a global financial shock, because in a world of interconnected markets, scale turns minor errors into systemic risks.

The responsibility of scale also extends to security. The infamous "Heartbleed" vulnerability, discovered in the widely used OpenSSL library, revealed how a flaw in open-source software maintained by a handful of volunteers could expose vast portions of the internet. Scale means that even neglected corners of code can become linchpins of global infrastructure.

But scale is not only a source of risk, it is a source of opportunity. The same reach that allows harm to spread can also spread good. Consider how open-source software empowers global collaboration, or how educational platforms scale knowledge to millions who would otherwise be excluded. When designed responsibly, software at scale can uplift entire generations.

The ethical imperative, then, is clear: engineers cannot retreat behind the excuse of being "just coders." To write code today is to wield global influence. Responsibility at this scale demands foresight, transparency, and courage. It demands that individuals and organizations pause to ask: If this reaches a billion users, what will the consequences be?

Future generations will judge us not only by the systems we created but by how responsibly we wielded their reach. In the age of scale, responsibility is not optional, it is the defining duty of our profession.

3. Designing With Foresight and Care

Ethics cannot be retrofitted. Once harm is baked into a system, it is often too late to undo its effects. Designing ethically requires foresight: the discipline of anticipating consequences, even unintended ones, and embedding safeguards from the start.

Foresight begins with questions. Instead of asking only how quickly we can deploy this feature? we must ask:

Who might be excluded or disadvantaged by this design?

What risks emerge if this scales globally?

How could this system be misused in ways we did not intend?

If this persists for decades, will it reflect values we are proud of?

This shift transforms design from short-term optimization into long-term stewardship. For example, when engineers design data collection systems, foresight means not only securing data today but also asking: How might future regimes misuse this data? Could it be weaponized against vulnerable groups? By asking such questions, engineers embed safeguards, limiting data retention, anonymizing sensitive information, or decentralizing storage.

Foresight also demands inclusivity. Systems designed only for majority users often fail marginalized groups, reinforcing exclusion. Consider early facial recognition systems that misidentified people of color at alarming rates. These failures were not only technical, but they were also ethical. A lack of diverse datasets and inclusive design processes encoded bias into systems that now shape law enforcement and commerce.

Care is the companion of foresight. Where foresight anticipates, care ensures empathy. To design with care is to remember that behind every line of code is a human life. It is to approach engineering not only as problem-solving but as relationship-building, with users, communities, and future generations.

Some frameworks for embedding foresight and care already exist. "Privacy by design" principles insist that privacy considerations be built into systems from the ground up. Ethical AI guidelines advocate for fairness, transparency, and accountability. Sustainability initiatives remind us that even algorithms carry environmental costs, energy-hungry training models, sprawling data centers, endless streams of computation.

But frameworks alone are not enough. What truly sustains foresight and care is culture. Organizations must cultivate environments where questioning is valued, dissent is welcomed, and ethical considerations are treated as essential design constraints. Engineers must feel empowered not only to ask Can we build this?" but also to insist Should we build this?

The cultural dimension is perhaps the most difficult. It requires slowing down in industries obsessed with speed. It requires resisting the pressure to cut corners for profit or deadlines. But it also yields the deepest rewards: systems that endure, that uplift, that leave legacies worth inheriting.

Future generations will not thank us for features shipped quickly or profits maximized in quarterly reports. They will thank us for the wisdom to pause, to foresee, to care. They will thank us for systems that do not simply function but also honor their humanity.

Closing Reflection

Ethics in code is not about constraint; it is about compass. Without ethics, technology may advance but drift, powerful yet hollow, innovative yet destructive. With ethics, technology becomes more than a tool; it becomes a legacy.

To design ethically is to acknowledge that we will never see the full consequences of our work. The systems we create may outlive us, shaping lives far beyond our reach. That is both a humbling truth and a profound responsibility.

Future generations will inherit our algorithms, our infrastructures, our values encoded in code. Let them inherit systems that reflect fairness, foresight, and care. Let them inherit not just functioning architectures but moral blueprints. For in the end, the greatest measure of tomorrow's software will not be its speed or efficiency but the humanity it preserves and uplifts.

Chapter 8

Education for Eternal Learners

In an age where the only constant is change, the very foundations of our digital world must be re-evaluated. The illusion of a stable, predictable future has been shattered by a cascade of unpredictable events: global pandemics, rapid climate shifts, and geopolitical instability. Within this new reality, software cannot afford to be fragile. The core tenet of modern design must be resilience a philosophy that embraces uncertainty as the norm and builds systems capable of bending without breaking. The provided text frames this challenge beautifully, arguing that resilience is not merely a technical objective but a profound ethical and philosophical one. It demands that we move beyond metrics of uptime and efficiency to a more fundamental question: will our systems continue to serve humanity when the world changes in ways we cannot possibly predict? This requires a radical shift in mindset, from building for a known, stable environment to creating infrastructures that are adaptable, durable, and, above all, human centered.

The Architecture of Anticipation: Embracing the Unexpected

The first principle of building resilient systems is a deep-seated humility. It is the recognition that we cannot, and will not, foresee every possible failure or disruption. The global pandemic of 2020 served as a brutal, real-time stress test for our digital infrastructure. Educational platforms, designed for a physical classroom world, crumbled under the weight of an unprecedented, simultaneous shift to remote learning. Global supply chain software, built on a model of just-in-time efficiency, lacked the flexibility to adapt to sudden disruptions in manufacturing and logistics. Healthcare systems, at the very moment they were most needed, proved to be a fragmented mess of incompatible data silos, making it nearly impossible to coordinate a coherent response. These were not minor hiccups; they were system-wide failures born from an over-reliance on a world that no longer existed.

The lesson is clear: anticipating the unexpected means designing with flexibility at the core. A rigid, monolithic architecture, no matter how efficient it is under ideal conditions, is inherently brittle. The alternative is a modular, decentralized design. In such an architecture, components are loosely coupled, allowing them to be replaced, updated, or scaled independently without causing a cascading failure of the entire system. Think of a system not as a single, massive engine, but as a collection of smaller, independent machines that can communicate and collaborate. If one machine fails, the others can pick up the slack, or a new machine can be swapped in without shutting down the entire operation. This approach to design, known as microservices, is a technical manifestation of the philosophical principle of humility; it assumes failure as an inevitable part of the process and builds pathways for graceful degradation instead of catastrophic collapse.

The text's metaphor of a natural ecosystem is particularly powerful here. Nature's resilience is not born from perfection but from diversity. A forest, with its wide variety of tree species, ground cover, and animal life, can withstand a disease that targets a single species. The ocean, with its complex food web, can recover from a localized disruption because life exists at multiple levels and in countless forms. In the same vein, a monoculture of digital systems where everyone relies on the same single platform, the same cloud provider, or the same programming language, is a recipe for large-scale, systemic fragility. A bug in that one platform could take down countless critical services. Resilience, therefore, requires a commitment to multiplicity: diversity of infrastructure, protocols, and design assumptions. It is a defense against a single point of failure and an investment in the long-term health of our digital ecosystem.

The Ethical Core: Human-Centered Continuity

Resilience in software is not an abstract technical problem; it is a human problem. A system that remains technically online during a crisis but fails to serve the people who depend on it is not truly resilient. This is the essence of human-centered continuity. It forces us to ask: how do our systems sustain not just their own operations but the well-being of the humans who rely on them? The answer requires a deep level of empathy to be embedded at the architectural level.

Consider a banking application during a major natural disaster. The server may be running perfectly, but if the user interface is complex and requires multiple steps to access emergency funds, it fails at the human level. An overwhelmed and stressed user, operating with limited battery life and a shaky internet connection, needs a simple, intuitive, and lightning-fast experience. A healthcare database, which may be a marvel of data science, is useless if its information retrieval process is too slow for a doctor trying to save a life in a chaotic emergency room. Building for human-centered continuity means designing interfaces for clarity under pressure. It means prioritizing the most essential information and making it instantly accessible, and it means building support systems that are built on the assumption that users in a crisis are stressed, distracted, and vulnerable.

Furthermore, a true commitment to human-centered resilience means addressing the profound inequalities that disasters and crises often magnify. Those with stable internet, reliable devices, and financial privilege are far better equipped to weather a storm than those without. The digital divide, which is a constant presence in times of peace, can become a chasm in times of crisis. Therefore, resilient systems for tomorrow cannot be designed solely for the best-case scenarios. Offline functionality must be a core design goal, allowing people to access critical information and services even when connectivity is lost. Low-bandwidth modes should be an integral part of the design, ensuring that systems are usable even with a slow and unreliable connection. And multilingual access and culturally sensitive design are not simply nice-to-haves; they are lifelines that ensure critical information reaches everyone, regardless of their background.

Ultimately, human-centered continuity transforms resilience from a technical objective into a moral one. It is a recognition that our systems have a responsibility to serve all of humanity, not just those with the best infrastructure. It is a commitment to building systems that are not just robust in the face of technical failure but compassionate in the face of human vulnerability. It ensures that when uncertainty strikes, our digital tools serve people first, not just the metrics of system uptime.

The Long View: Designing for Generational Durability

The final and perhaps most daunting challenge of resilience is durability: the ability of a system to not just survive a single crisis but to sustain its relevance and utility across decades of unpredictable change. In the transient world of modern software, this is a radical concept. We live in an era of planned obsolescence, where products are designed for short lifespans, updates break compatibility, and communities are constantly urged to migrate to the "next big thing." This short-termism is the ultimate enemy of resilience and a profound disservice to future generations.

To design for generational durability requires a fundamental shift in perspective. We must begin to see our software not as disposable products but as living infrastructure, akin to the roads, bridges, and energy grids that we expect to last for a century or more. This means making a conscious effort to build systems that can evolve with society, with technology, and with the changing needs of humanity. One of the most critical aspects of this is documentation for posterity. We must move beyond documenting code for the next developer and begin to document it for the student who will study it fifty years from now. This means explaining not just the "how" but also the "why" of the architectural decisions, the ethical considerations, and the original intent behind the system. This kind of historical record is a gift that ensures our work can be understood, adapted, and built upon long after its creators are gone.

Furthermore, durability requires a commitment to open standards and interoperability. Closed, proprietary systems, no matter how innovative they are today, create a lock-in that makes them brittle and difficult to maintain over time. An open system, with clearly defined standards and protocols, allows for a multiplicity of implementations and ensures that it can be a part of a larger, evolving ecosystem. Think of the durability of the Internet Protocol (IP), which has remained the fundamental standard for data transfer for decades, allowing countless new technologies to be built on top of it. This is the model for generational durability.

Finally, durability requires a deep ecological awareness. A system that is technically resilient but requires a massive amount of energy to operate is ultimately a fragile system. It is vulnerable to energy crises and contributes to the very climate change that is creating so much of the uncertainty in our world. Resilient software must be sustainable in its resource consumption, recognizing that true resilience is about not just the continuity of a single system but the continuity of the planet itself.

In conclusion, resilient systems are not fortresses built to resist every storm; they are dynamic, adaptable ecosystems designed to recover and grow in the face of uncertainty. They are built with humility, designed with empathy, and crafted with an eye toward the distant future. In a world defined by turbulence, resilience is the greatest gift we can leave behind. It is a promise that our systems will not shatter under pressure, that they will serve people in times of crisis, and that they will endure long enough to become the foundation for futures we cannot yet imagine. To design for resilience is to design with faith in humanity's endurance to acknowledge uncertainty while refusing to succumb to fragility. It is, ultimately, to weave a sense of permanence into a transient world.

Chapter 9

Balancing Automation and Humanity

The story of technology is often told as a relentless march toward automation, where machines gradually take over tasks once performed by human hands, algorithms step in to make decisions that were once the domain of human intellect, and intricate systems assume the oversight roles that people have traditionally held. This narrative paints a picture of progress as an inevitable progression from manual labor to mechanical efficiency, from human error to algorithmic precision. Yet, with every advancement in this direction, a profound and fundamental question arises: what aspects of our existence remain uniquely and irreplaceably human? In an era where artificial intelligence and robotics are evolving at an unprecedented pace, the software of tomorrow must do more than simply automate processes with flawless efficiency. It must also preserve the essence of humanity in a meaningful way, ensuring that technological progress enhances rather than erodes the human experience.

Automation holds an undeniable allure because it promises unparalleled speed, unerring precision, and the ability to scale operations far beyond what any individual or group of humans could achieve alone. Imagine factories churning out products at rates that dwarf human capabilities, or data centers processing billions of transactions in seconds without a single mistake. These promises are not mere hype; they have transformed industries, boosted economies, and solved problems that once seemed insurmountable. However, when pursued without restraint, automation carries significant risks. It can erode human dignity by rendering people obsolete in their own workplaces, displace workers without providing new avenues for purpose and fulfillment, and ultimately reduce human beings to passive spectators in societies that they once actively shaped. The challenge for designers, engineers, and policymakers is to create software that endures not just through technical robustness but through its harmonious integration with human values. To achieve this, we must resist the seductive temptation to maximize automation at any cost, particularly when it comes at the expense of our shared humanity. Instead, the true balance lies in constructing systems where automation serves as an amplifier of human capacity rather than a diminisher of it, where technology functions not as a cold replacement for people but as a collaborative partner that elevates their potential.

This chapter explores this delicate equilibrium in depth, examining how automation can be reimagined as a force for amplification rather than substitution, the necessity of implementing robust ethical guardrails to prevent misuse, and the importance of fostering a symbiotic relationship between humans and machines. By delving into these areas with detailed examples, historical insights, and forward-looking considerations, we can chart a path toward software design that honors both technological innovation and human integrity. Ultimately, the goal is to ensure that future generations inherit a world where automation enriches lives rather than impoverishing the human spirit.

Amplifying Human Potential Through Automation

At the heart of the automation debate lies a critical peril: the tendency to view humans as mere impediments to operational efficiency. When technological systems are engineered with the primary aim of circumventing human involvement altogether, we inadvertently undermine the very skills, intuitions, and judgments that have long fortified societies against uncertainty and adversity. Consider the historical precedent of the Industrial Revolution, where mechanized looms and assembly lines displaced artisans and laborers, leading to widespread social upheaval, including the Luddite rebellions. While those machines brought about economic growth, they also hollowed out communities by devaluing craftsmanship without immediately offering alternative paths for human endeavor. Today, as we stand on the cusp of even more advanced automation driven by machine learning and robotics, we must learn from this history to avoid repeating its mistakes.

Rather than positioning automation as a direct replacement for human labor, it should be conceptualized as a powerful tool for amplification. This shift in perspective transforms technology from an adversary into an ally. For instance, in the field of medicine, a physician equipped with sophisticated diagnostic algorithms can analyze patient data at speeds and accuracies that surpass human capabilities alone. These tools can sift through vast medical databases, identify patterns in symptoms, and suggest potential diagnoses based on probabilistic models trained on millions of cases. However, the irreplaceable elements of care, such as empathy in communicating a difficult prognosis, the nuanced understanding of a patient's cultural background, or the ethical weighing of treatment options in light of personal values, remain firmly in the human domain. By automating the rote analysis, the doctor is freed to focus on these higher-order aspects, leading to better patient outcomes and a more fulfilling professional experience.

Similarly, in education, teachers burdened by administrative tasks like grading essays or tracking student progress can benefit immensely from AI-driven tools. An automated grading system might evaluate grammar, structure, and factual accuracy with objective precision, processing hundreds of assignments in the time it takes a human to handle a handful. This liberation from paperwork allows educators to dedicate more energy to nurturing creativity, mentoring students through personal challenges, and designing innovative lesson plans that spark intellectual curiosity. The result is not a diminished role for the teacher but an enhanced one, where human ingenuity is amplified to foster deeper learning environments.

This amplification approach inherently preserves human agency, the sense of control and purposeful action that is essential to individual well-being and societal resilience. It acknowledges a fundamental dichotomy: machines excel at computation, pattern recognition, and repetitive tasks, handling volumes of data with tireless efficiency. Humans, on the other hand, thrive in realms of meaning-making, where ambiguity, emotion, and ethical considerations come into play. For example, in legal professions, AI can review contracts for compliance issues or predict case outcomes based on precedents, but the interpretation of justice in a specific cultural or moral context requires human insight. The objective of automation, therefore, should not be to relegate humans to mere overseers of autonomous systems, monitoring dashboards while machines make all the decisions. Instead, it should elevate humans into roles that leverage their unique strengths: interpreting complex narratives, navigating ethical dilemmas, unleashing creativity in problem-solving, and providing compassionate care in interpersonal interactions.

To illustrate this further, let's examine the aviation industry. Autopilot systems have revolutionized flying by handling routine aspects of navigation, altitude control, and fuel management, reducing pilot fatigue and error rates. Yet, pilots remain central, ready to intervene in emergencies, make judgment calls during turbulence, or adapt to unforeseen variables like weather changes. This model of amplification has made air travel safer without eliminating the need for human expertise; in fact, it has heightened the value of pilots' training and intuition. Extending this principle to software design, we must prioritize interfaces that empower users, providing tools that augment rather than automate away human input. Adaptive algorithms that learn from user feedback, customizable automation workflows that allow personalization, and systems with built-in "human-in-the-loop" mechanisms all contribute to this amplification ethos.

When we commit to designing systems that amplify human capabilities, we affirm that technology's ultimate purpose is not to achieve independence from humanity but to foster a profound interdependence with it. This interdependence ensures that as machines grow more capable, humans do not become obsolete but instead evolve into more sophisticated versions of themselves. In the long term, this approach builds resilient societies where technological progress supports human flourishing, preventing the dystopian scenarios where automation leads to widespread unemployment or social disconnection. By embedding amplification as a core principle in software architecture, from user experience design to algorithmic logic, we can create enduring technologies that adapt to human needs rather than forcing humans to adapt to them.

Establishing Ethical Boundaries for Automation

Without proper oversight, automation can veer into dangerous territory, amplifying existing societal flaws rather than alleviating them. History is replete with examples where unchecked technological deployment has led to unintended consequences. For instance, early facial recognition systems, automated for efficiency in security applications, often exhibited biases against certain ethnic groups due to skewed training data, perpetuating discrimination in law enforcement. Surveillance technologies, designed to enhance safety, have sometimes eroded privacy rights, turning public spaces into zones of constant monitoring without consent. Even more alarmingly, the development of autonomous weapons systems raises the specter of machines making life-and-death decisions in warfare, detached from human moral accountability. These cases underscore the perils of automation devoid of ethical constraints, highlighting the need for deliberate boundaries to safeguard human values.

To ensure ethical automation, designers and developers must proactively establish explicit guardrails that address potential harms from the outset. This begins with a rigorous examination of which tasks should never be fully automated, recognizing that some domains demand the irreplaceable nuance of human involvement. For example, end-of-life decisions in healthcare, such as determining when to withdraw life support, involve profound ethical, emotional, and familial considerations that no algorithm can fully encapsulate. Similarly, in judiciary systems, while AI can assist in researching precedents or predicting recidivism risks, the final sentencing must incorporate human judgment to account for rehabilitation potential, societal context, and mercy, elements that defy purely data-driven logic.

Equally important is identifying areas where human judgment must remain central, even as automation handles peripheral tasks. In creative industries like journalism, algorithms might curate news feeds or fact-check articles, but the core act of investigative reporting, building sources, interpreting motives, and crafting narratives that resonate with truth requires human oversight to maintain integrity and avoid misinformation. Automation in these spaces should support, not supplant, the human element, ensuring that decisions with significant social impact are vetted by people who can weigh broader implications.

Furthermore, a key focus must be on how to ensure that automation reflects fairness rather than amplifying existing biases. Bias in AI often stems from unrepresentative datasets or flawed training processes, leading to outcomes that disadvantage marginalized groups. To counter this, developers should implement diverse data sourcing, regular audits for equity, and mechanisms for bias detection and correction. For instance, in hiring algorithms used by companies to screen resumes, incorporating fairness constraints, such as equalizing selection rates across demographics, can prevent the perpetuation of historical inequalities. Transparency in how these systems operate is crucial; users and stakeholders should have access to explanations of algorithmic decisions, fostering trust and enabling challenges when biases emerge.

These guardrails are not intended to stifle innovation but to channel it toward outcomes that uphold human dignity. Essential features like transparency, where systems provide clear rationales for their actions, accountability, through traceable logs and responsible parties, and human override capabilities, allowing intervention in critical moments, must be integrated into the core architecture of automated systems. Take self-driving cars as an example: an autonomous vehicle should not only navigate roads but also log and explain decisions, such as why it chose to swerve left during an obstacle avoidance maneuver. This allows for post-event analysis and learning, while human passengers or operators retain the ability to take control if needed. In financial sectors, algorithms that assess loan applications must include provisions for human review, especially in borderline cases, to prevent automated denials that could exacerbate economic disparities based on flawed credit models.

Ethical automation also demands resistance to the economic pressures that prioritize short-term profits over long-term human flourishing. Corporations may be tempted to automate jobs en masse to cut costs, but this can lead to societal costs like increased inequality and mental health crises among displaced workers. Instead, the true measure of technological progress should be how much it expands human potential through reskilling programs, new job creation in emerging fields, or enhanced leisure time for personal growth. Policymakers can support this by enacting regulations that incentivize ethical practices, such as tax benefits for companies that maintain human-centered automation or mandates for impact assessments before deploying large-scale systems.

By embedding these guardrails, we protect against a future where efficiency eclipses empathy, ensuring that automation serves as a benevolent force. This proactive stance not only mitigates risks but also builds public confidence in technology, paving the way for broader adoption and innovation. In essence, ethical boundaries transform automation from a potential threat into a trusted tool, aligned with the values that define our humanity.

Fostering Symbiotic Partnerships Between Humans and Machines

The narrative of the future should not be framed as an adversarial contest between humans and machines, where one must inevitably dominate the other. Rather, it should envision a collaborative paradigm: humans working in tandem with machines, each leveraging their strengths to achieve outcomes neither could accomplish alone. This symbiotic relationship requires intentional design, where systems are built to facilitate mutual learning, adaptation, and co-creation, fostering a dynamic partnership that evolves over time.

Achieving symbiosis begins with humility on both sides of the equation. Machines must be programmed to acknowledge the boundaries of their capabilities, incorporating uncertainty estimates in their outputs or flagging scenarios where human input is advisable. For example, in predictive analytics for weather forecasting, AI models can provide probabilistic predictions but should highlight limitations in chaotic systems, prompting meteorologists to apply their experiential knowledge. Conversely, humans must embrace the idea that automation can extend their perceptual and cognitive horizons without undermining their authority. This mindset shift is crucial in fields like scientific research, where AI can simulate millions of molecular interactions to accelerate drug discovery, but researchers retain the role of hypothesizing, experimenting, and interpreting results in the context of broader scientific paradigms.

In practice, this partnership manifests vividly in creative domains, where the interplay between human intuition and machine computation yields extraordinary results. Musicians, for instance, can employ AI tools to generate novel melodies or harmonic progressions based on stylistic inputs, exploring sonic landscapes that might take years to discover manually. Yet, it is the artist's personal touch infusing the composition with emotional depth, cultural references, or improvisational flair that transforms these generated elements into meaningful art. Similarly, architects utilize generative algorithms to produce thousands of structural variations optimized for sustainability and aesthetics, but the final selection hinges on human criteria like cultural resonance, community integration, and symbolic significance. These collaborations demonstrate how machines expand the creative canvas, providing raw material and inspiration while humans imbue it with soul and purpose.

To design symbiosis effectively, foresight is essential. Future systems should avoid trapping users in passive roles, such as merely consuming algorithmically curated content on social media platforms. Instead, they should invite active participation through interactive interfaces that encourage exploration and customization. For example, educational software could adapt to a student's learning style while allowing them to query the system, suggest modifications, or even contribute to its knowledge base, turning users into co-creators. This dialogic approach where humans and machines exchange feedback in real time strengthens the bond, making technology feel like an extension of the self rather than an external imposition.

Moreover, symbiotic design must address accessibility and inclusivity, ensuring that these partnerships benefit diverse populations. For individuals with disabilities, AI-powered prosthetics or voice assistants can amplify physical or communicative abilities, but true symbiosis involves user-configurable adaptations that evolve with personal needs. In workplace settings, collaborative robots (cobots) in manufacturing lines work alongside humans, handling heavy lifting while adapting to human-paced workflows, reducing injury risks, and enhancing productivity without displacement.

By prioritizing symbiosis, we cultivate a future where humans and machines complement each other seamlessly: machines offering scalability and consistency, and humans providing ethical guidance and innovative leaps. This harmonious integration not only maximizes efficiency but also enriches the human experience, ensuring that technological advancement aligns with our deepest aspirations.

The quest to balance automation and humanity stands as one of the most pivotal dilemmas of our era, shaping not just the trajectory of technology but the very fabric of society. If we pursue automation with reckless abandon, driven solely by the allure of efficiency and profit, we hazard constructing a world where humans become superfluous, relegated to the margins of a machine-dominated existence. Conversely, if we outright reject automation in fear of its disruptions, we forfeit the immense potential to augment our collective capabilities, solve pressing global challenges, and unlock new realms of possibility. The enlightened path forward demands a nuanced equilibrium: automation that thoughtfully amplifies human strengths, robust guardrails that vigilantly protect against ethical pitfalls, and a commitment to symbiosis that celebrates the enduring partnership between people and their creations.

For the generations that will inherit this technological landscape, the central inquiry will transcend the mere feasibility of machines supplanting humans. Instead, it will probe whether humans have the wisdom to safeguard those qualities that are intrinsically irreplaceable our capacity for empathy, moral reasoning, and transcendent creativity. Automation, for all its formidable power, must always be directed by the compass of humanity, ensuring that progress serves life rather than subjugating it. In the endeavor to craft tomorrow's software, the pinnacle of success will not lie in developing systems that operate autonomously, free from human touch. Rather, it will be realized in creating technologies that thrive in concert with us, magnifying our inventive spirit, upholding our inherent dignity, and guaranteeing that within every automated sequence, the rich tapestry of the human narrative continues to radiate with undiminished brilliance.

Chapter 10

The Legacy We Leave Behind

Every generation builds with materials it inherits and leaves behind structures for the next. In the physical world, these legacies are bridges, libraries, and monuments tangible artifacts that stand as testaments to human ingenuity and perseverance. Bridges span rivers and connect communities, enduring floods and earthquakes if built with foresight. Libraries house the accumulated wisdom of ages, their shelves groaning under the weight of books that preserve stories, ideas, and discoveries. Monuments rise skyward, commemorating triumphs, tragedies, and the indomitable spirit of those who came before. These physical inheritances shape the landscapes we inhabit, influencing how we move, learn, and remember.

In the digital world, however, our legacies are both more fragile and more expansive. They consist of lines of code that power applications, protocols that govern data flow, networks that link billions of devices, and communities that form around shared digital spaces. Unlike stone or steel, these digital constructs can vanish in an instant due to a server shutdown, a corporate bankruptcy, or a simple update that renders them obsolete. Yet, their reach is unparalleled; a single algorithm can influence global elections, a platform can redefine social interactions for entire populations, and a piece of open-source software can evolve into the backbone of industries. These legacies do not merely shape physical spaces, they redefine how future generations live, create, and connect on a planetary scale.

As software architects of today, we do not merely write code; we write the scaffolding of tomorrow's civilization. Our systems will outlast us in ways we cannot always predict, embedding themselves into the fabric of daily life long after we've moved on. A poorly designed algorithm, for instance, might perpetuate biases in hiring processes, echoing harm for decades through automated decisions that disadvantage certain groups. Conversely, a thoughtfully crafted platform, like an open educational resource, could empower generations of learners and dreamers, providing access to knowledge that sparks innovation and social mobility. The question is not whether we leave a legacy; every line of code contributes to one, but what kind of legacy we choose to leave. Do we prioritize fleeting trends, or do we build with an eye toward enduring impact?

The work of this era is not only about building for efficiency or convenience, though those are important drivers in a fast-paced tech landscape. It is about building for continuity, responsibility, and meaning qualities that ensure our creations serve humanity beyond the immediate horizon. Efficiency might optimize a supply chain today, but continuity ensures that the chain adapts to tomorrow's disruptions. Convenience might streamline a user interface, but responsibility guards against unintended harms like privacy breaches that erode trust over time. Meaning elevates technology from a tool to a catalyst for human potential, reminding us that innovation should foster connection, creativity, and equity. The legacy we leave behind is not measured in downloads, user metrics, or quarterly profits, but in the lives touched, the barriers broken, and the futures enabled. It is in the student who discovers a passion through an accessible app, the activist who mobilizes a movement via a secure network, or the researcher who builds upon our code to solve a pressing global challenge.

In this chapter, we explore the multifaceted nature of digital legacy through three lenses: building for continuity, responsibility across generations, and planting seeds of meaning. Each aspect invites us to reflect on our role as stewards of technology, urging us to design not just for the now, but for the unknowable then.

Building for Continuity

Continuity is the thread that carries knowledge, culture, and progress across generations, much like how ancient languages such as Latin evolved into modern Romance tongues, preserving philosophical and scientific ideas through millennia. Philosophies from thinkers like Aristotle continue to influence ethics and logic today, while epic stories like the Iliad or the Mahabharata endure as cultural touchstones, adapted into films, books, and digital media. In software, continuity means aspiring to this same endurance, creating systems that persist and evolve rather than fade into irrelevance. It requires resisting the allure of short-termism, the pressure to chase viral trends, quick monetization, or hype-driven features that prioritize immediate gratification over long-term viability.

Building for continuity involves designing systems that can adapt to new contexts, much like how biological ecosystems evolve in response to environmental changes. This means incorporating modular architectures where components can be updated independently, using standard protocols that allow interoperability, and documenting code with clarity so that future developers can understand and extend it without starting from scratch. When original creators are gone, retired, moved on, or passed away, the system must remain interpretable, with comments, wikis, and version histories serving as guides. Obsolescence is a constant threat in tech; hardware advances, languages fall out of favor, and dependencies break. To counter this, continuity demands forward-thinking choices, such as avoiding proprietary lock-ins that tie a system's fate to a single vendor or embracing backward compatibility to ensure older data and integrations remain functional.

Consider the stark difference between disposable apps and enduring infrastructures. Disposable apps, like those fleeting social media fads that rise and fall with cultural whims, think of platforms that mimic TikTok's short-form videos but lack unique value, often disappear within five years, leaving behind broken connections, lost data, and frustrated users who must migrate elsewhere. Users invest time building profiles, curating content, and forming networks, only to see it all evaporate when investor funding dries up or market saturation hits. In contrast, an open protocol like HTTP, which underpins the web itself, has sustained and maintained relevance for decades. Developed in the early 1990s, it outlived dial-up modems, early browsers, and even the companies that first championed it, evolving through versions like HTTP/2 and HTTP/3 to handle modern demands such as mobile streaming and security. This endurance stems from its open nature, allowing global collaboration and adaptation.

Another exemplar is the Linux kernel, initiated by Linus Torvalds in 1991 as a hobby project. Today, it powers everything from supercomputers to smartphones, outlasting proprietary operating systems that once dominated. Its continuity arises from a community-driven model, where thousands of contributors ensure it adapts to new hardware, security threats, and use cases. This humility in design, acknowledging that we are not the final users, is crucial. Others will come after us with different needs, perhaps integrating AI in ways we can't foresee, or scaling to handle quantum computing. By building with extensibility in mind, using APIs that invite plugins, or data formats that are human-readable we honor this.

The greatest legacy we can leave is not perfection, an unattainable ideal in a field riddled with bugs and evolving requirements, but adaptability. Systems that bend rather than break, like flexible bridges engineered to sway in high winds, become the invisible architecture upon which futures can be built. Think of how email protocols have adapted from simple text exchanges to multimedia-rich communications, surviving the rise of instant messaging and social networks. Or consider blockchain protocols like Bitcoin's, which, despite criticisms, have inspired a wave of decentralized applications that redefine finance and ownership. These examples illustrate that continuity isn't about stasis; it's about creating foundations that invite iteration.

To achieve this, software architects must cultivate practices like rigorous testing for edge cases, investing in automated migration tools for data longevity, and fostering open-source ecosystems where knowledge isn't siloed. Education plays a role too mentoring the next generation through code reviews, conferences, and shared repositories ensures skills transfer. In a world where tech cycles accelerate, building for continuity is an act of defiance against obsolescence, ensuring our digital bridges don't collapse under the weight of time.

Responsibility Across Generations

Legacy extends beyond the technical realm into the moral, where every line of code carries ethical weight. To design for tomorrow is to accept responsibility for people we may never meet future users, communities, and even entire societies shaped by our choices. This intergenerational duty demands a shift from reactive fixes to proactive foresight, anticipating how today's decisions might unfold over decades.

Responsibility across generations begins with probing questions that pierce the veil of immediacy: Will this system cause harm decades from now, perhaps through accumulated data that enables surveillance states or manipulative AI? Will it amplify inequalities, like algorithms that favor affluent users in loan approvals, or bridge them by prioritizing accessibility features for the disabled? Will it exhaust resources, such as energy-hungry data centers contributing to climate change, or steward them through efficient, green computing practices? Will it prioritize short-term gain, like addictive features that boost engagement metrics at the cost of mental health, over long-term well-being that promotes balanced digital lives?

The responsibility of software creators is unique because of the scale and speed of digital impact. Unlike physical tools of the past, a hammer that affects one craftsman or a bridge that serves a local community, digital legacies spread instantly and endure invisibly. A single decision, such as how an algorithm ranks information on a search engine, can shape public discourse for generations, influencing what knowledge is accessible and how opinions form. Google's PageRank, for instance, revolutionized information retrieval but also inadvertently amplified echo chambers by prioritizing popular links. Similarly, how a database handles identity through centralized servers vulnerable to hacks or decentralized systems like self-sovereign identities can affect billions, determining vulnerability to identity theft or empowerment through privacy control.

This scale amplifies ethical dilemmas. Consider social media platforms: early designs optimized for virality without robust moderation led to misinformation epidemics, as seen in events like the 2016 U.S. elections or the COVID-19 infodemic. These ripples continue, eroding trust in institutions and polarizing societies. Environmental responsibility is equally pressing; the carbon footprint of training large language models rivals that of entire countries, raising questions about sustainable AI. Future generations, facing exacerbated climate crises, will judge us not just on innovation but on whether we mitigated these costs through renewable energy integrations or efficient algorithms.

To carry this responsibility, designers must embed ethical frameworks into the development lifecycle. This includes conducting impact assessments that simulate long-term effects, diverse teams to uncover blind spots, and transparent audits that allow public scrutiny. Regulations like the EU's GDPR set precedents for data privacy, forcing companies to build consent mechanisms that endure beyond product lifecycles. Open-source initiatives, such as those from the Electronic Frontier Foundation, provide tools for privacy-preserving tech, ensuring responsibility isn't gatekept by corporations.

Restraint is key, knowing when not to build. The "move fast and break things" mantra, once celebrated, now reveals its flaws in broken trust and societal fractures. Instead, adopt "move thoughtfully and mend futures," prioritizing user agency, inclusivity, and sustainability. For instance, designing AI with explainability ensures future users can interrogate decisions, preventing opaque "black boxes" that perpetuate injustice. In healthcare software, responsibility means safeguarding patient data against breaches that could haunt individuals for life.

Ultimately, future generations will not only use our systems, but they will also judge us by them, scrutinizing whether we wield power with care. By embracing this, we transform software from a neutral tool into a force for good, ensuring our digital inheritance enriches rather than burdens.

Planting Seeds of Meaning

Legacy transcends functionality and ethics to encompass meaning, the deeper purpose that infuses technology with soul. The systems we leave behind should not only function efficiently or responsibly; they should inspire, evoking wonder and reminding future generations that technology was never just about efficiency but about human flourishing. Meaning turns code into a narrative, a story of aspiration that connects creators to inheritors.

Planting seeds of meaning requires embedding values deliberately into design, much like how architects infuse buildings with symbolism, cathedrals soaring to inspire awe, or public parks designed for communal reflection. In software, open-source projects embody collaboration, as seen in GitHub repositories where global contributors co-create, fostering a sense of shared ownership. Educational platforms like Khan Academy embody generosity, offering free access to knowledge that democratizes learning, planting seeds that bloom into empowered minds worldwide. Inclusive systems, such as voice assistants with multilingual support or apps with screen reader compatibility, embody dignity, affirming that technology serves all humanity, not just the privileged few.

These are not technical accidents but deliberate choices that carry forward the spirit of their creators. Meaning arises from intention: prioritizing user well-being over addictive loops, as in apps that encourage mindful usage with digital wellness features. Or embedding sustainability, like software that optimizes energy use in smart grids, aligning tech with planetary health. Meaningful legacy isn't about grandeur, massive platforms like Facebook, while influential, often generate fleeting distraction through endless scrolls. Instead, it's about care in the small things: a tool that enables a remote village to monitor clean water sources via IoT sensors, potentially saving lives and fostering self-reliance. This modest intervention may outshine viral apps in lasting impact, helping communities thrive amid challenges like climate-induced droughts.

The question is not how much we build, quantity of features or lines of code, but whether what we build helps humanity move closer to wisdom, justice, and imagination. Wisdom through systems that promote critical thinking, like AI tutors that encourage questioning over rote answers. Justice via platforms that amplify marginalized voices, countering historical biases in media. Imagination in creative tools like open-source 3D modeling software that lets dreamers prototype inventions without barriers.

Seeds of meaning do not bloom instantly; they require patience and faith. Planted in a codebase today, they might germinate years later when a young developer forks a project to address a new crisis, like adapting educational software for refugee camps. Our role is not to complete the story, technology evolves too rapidly for that, but to ensure the story continues, providing fertile ground through documentation, licensing, and community building.

In cultivating meaning, we draw from diverse inspirations: art, philosophy, and nature. Analogies to gardens remind us that software ecosystems need nurturing, pruning bugs, watering with updates, and enriching with diverse contributions. By doing so, we create legacies that resonate emotionally, inspiring successors to build with the same care.

As we close this blueprint for tomorrow, one truth rises above all others: software is not just code; it is a legacy, a bridge between generations, a canvas of responsibility, and a garden of meaning. What we design today will shape the possibilities of those who come after us, influencing how they collaborate, innovate, and confront challenges. The systems we inherit were built by imperfect hands early internet pioneers grappling with limited bandwidth, or database architects navigating ethical gray areas, yet they carried us here, enabling the connected world we take for granted. The systems we leave behind will also be imperfect, riddled with trade-offs and unforeseen flaws, yet they will carry others forward, provided we infuse them with intention.

The measure of our era will not be whether we built flawless systems perfection is a myth in an ever-changing field but whether we built with care, foresight, and humanity. Care in the details that make tech humane, foresight in anticipating ripples, and humanity in centering people over profits. Our legacy is not written only in repositories or data centers it is written in the lives made fuller through accessible tools, the voices amplified by equitable platforms, and the futures unlocked by innovative foundations. To design software for generations ahead is to see ourselves not as owners of tomorrow, but as stewards of its beginnings, humbly contributing to a continuum of progress.

And so, the question each of us must ask is simple but profound: What will we leave behind? In answering it, we define not just our work, but our place in the unfolding story of human endeavor.